"One of the hallmarks of Jesus's
'metanoia' or conversion. In this wide-ranging ...
Bonnette looks at how our conversion of heart must always be at
once directed towards God and directed out towards our fellow
human beings. With stories from her own life as a Catholic woman
(and scholar and mother and friend), she offers a book that is that
rare combination of superb scholarship and warm personal stories.
Highly recommended."

—JAMES MARTIN, SJ, Author of *Learning to Pray: A Guide for Everyone*

"Written with keen perspective, wit, love, and an open heart for
healing that caresses a genuine quest for reconciliation, Kathleen
Bonnette invites us to enter a true revolution today, where together,
we can build a better tomorrow with grace. This is an engaging
book. A serious adventure for justice."

—PATRICK SAINT-JEAN, SJ, author of *Home-Going: The Journey from
Racism and Death to Community and Hope*

"Kathleen Bonnette is no fan of the hierarchal paradigm for the *ordo
amoris* or the love that renders the cosmos a place of belonging. Hierarchies put people into their proper places. In what she advocates—
a relational ethic with cosmic overtones—propriety honors love's
inventiveness. But Bonnette doesn't just pit restless against rooted.
She explores, together with her School Sisters, the art of relating
to what resists relationship. This proves to be a bravely confessional
venture."

—JAMES WETZEL, author of *Parting Knowledge: Essays after Augustine*

"A holy thought not only can save you, but also can help sanctify the
world. Kathleen Bonette's theological exploration is a very thought-
ful and faithful journey towards that objective. Her academic prose
elevates this work."

—GLORIA PURVIS, host of *The Gloria Purvis Podcast*

"Kathleen Bonnette's beautifully written book invites readers on a journey to wholeness. She deftly uses her own story, the experiences of women religious, and the wisdom of Augustine to remind us that we are created for communion. Despite attempts by many to divide us, to deny the essence of trinitarian love, Bonnette encourages us to embrace the great mystery: We are one in the abundance of God. *Revolutionary Hope* is the perfect companion for all those on the journey: justice seekers, meaning makers, and all who long to know God who is loving us into wholeness."

—ANN SCHOLZ, SSND, former associate director for social mission, Leadership Conference of Women Religious

(R)evolutionary Hope

(R)evolutionary Hope

A Spirituality of Encounter and Engagement in an Evolving World

KATHLEEN BONNETTE

Foreword by Ilia Delio

CASCADE *Books* · Eugene, Oregon

REVOLUTIONARY HOPE
A Spirituality of Encounter and Engagement in an Evolving World

Copyright © 2023 Kathleen Bonnette. All rights reserved. Except for brief quotations in critical publications or reviews, no part of this book may be reproduced in any manner without prior written permission from the publisher. Write: Permissions, Wipf and Stock Publishers, 199 W. 8th Ave., Suite 3, Eugene, OR 97401.

Cascade Books
An Imprint of Wipf and Stock Publishers
199 W. 8th Ave., Suite 3
Eugene, OR 97401

www.wipfandstock.com

PAPERBACK ISBN: 978-1-6667-5203-8
HARDCOVER ISBN: 978-1-6667-5204-5
EBOOK ISBN: 978-1-6667-5205-2

Cataloguing-in-Publication data:

Names: Bonnette, Kathleen, author. | Delio, Ilia, foreword.

Title: Revolutionary hope : a spirituality of encounter and engagement in an evolving world / Kathleen Bonnette ; foreword by Ilia Delio.

Description: Eugene, OR : Cascade Books, 2023 | Includes bibliographical references.

Identifiers: ISBN 978-1-6667-5203-8 (paperback) | ISBN 978-1-6667-5204-5 (hardcover) | ISBN 978-1-6667-5205-2 (ebook)

Subjects: LCSH: Spirituality—Catholic Church. | Augustine, of Hippo, Saint, 354–430. | Evolution—Religious aspects—Catholic Church. | Cosmology. | School Sisters of Notre Dame.

Classification: BT701.3 .B66 2023 (paperback) | BT701.3 .B66 (ebook)

08/07/23

In honor of Arlene Flaherty, OP, and the SSND Community,
and to my mother and grandmothers,
who led the way.

And—always—for Dan, Elena, Caleb, and Erin.

The search—
for self,
for wisdom,
for love,
for truth,
for justice,
for God—
is strenuous and unending.
We need good companions
in order to persevere in it.
In good company,
in a community of conviction,
the quest never loses its
relevance,
its urgency,
or its savor.

—Kaye Ashe, OP[1]

1. "The Search," by Sister Kaye Ashe, OP, reprinted with permission from Sinsinawa Dominicans, Inc., www.sinsinawa.org.

Contents

Foreword

THIS IS A BEAUTIFUL book in every way. It is timely in its message, provocative in its depth, and forward-looking in its vision. Kathleen Bonnette offers profound insights based on Saint Augustine's question, "What do I love when I love my God?" The answer to this question, as Bonnette shows, is none other than the personal conversion of our lives. For the God of our heart's desire is the deepest center within. The author candidly speaks from her own experience, seasoned by a breadth of theological knowledge, but also from a wellspring of faith, a faith-filled hope that this world can be made new, if we take up the challenge of our spiritual growth. This book will be attractive to a wide range of people, but especially to younger generations who are searching for personal meaning and identity. I highly recommend it.

Sr. Ilia Delio, OSF
Josephine C. Connelly Endowed Chair in Theology
Villanova University

Acknowledgments

INSOFAR AS IT IS a reflection of my faith journey thus far, this book owes its existence to those who have been companions along the way:

First, I am grateful to the members of the Augustinian Institute at Villanova University, who recognized the potential of my project and offered me funding to explore the thesis through the Imbesi Family St. Augustine Fellowship. Jim Wetzel, Fr. Allan Fitzgerald, Ian Clausen, Paul Camacho, and Anna Monserrate—thank you for welcoming me, and for reading drafts and challenging me to think more deeply or expand my imaginative horizons. Your support for and interest in my work has been a source of great encouragement, and I am deeply grateful to have had the chance to learn from you and enjoy your friendship.

I am grateful, too, for all the delightful people I met or reconnected with at Villanova, particularly Mark Doorley, Kaley Carpenter, Kathryn Getek Soltis, and especially Sr. Ilia Delio, who generously agreed to read an early draft of this book and to write the foreword.

Veronica Ogle, Erika Kidd, Sr. Ann Scholz, Sr. Sharon Kanis, Sr. Kay O'Connell, Fr. Mike McDermott, Monsignor Murphy, Jayne Wilcox—thank you for taking the time to reflect on drafts of this project and for sharing your wisdom with me.

To the editorial team at Wipf and Stock: thank you for your commitment to this project and your skillful guidance that brought it to publication.

I am also grateful for the editors at *America: The Jesuit Review* and *U.S. Catholic*, who gave me a platform to explore many of these themes before bringing them all together in this book.

Sr. Arlene Flaherty is especially deserving of my thanks, as well. I had the privilege of serving for more than three years as her assistant director in the Office of Justice, Peace, and Integrity of Creation with the School Sisters of Notre Dame, Atlantic-Midwest Province. Her unflagging vivacity, determination, and fierce, faith-filled love in the face of injustice continue to challenge and inspire me. She enthusiastically read through many drafts of this text and her insights have informed this work profoundly. I am grateful for her oft-repeated exhortation to "keep writing."

To all the sisters, associates, and staff of the School Sisters of Notre Dame: you will never know the extent of my esteem for you, nor the importance of your influence on my faith life, but I hope this book gives you some indication. Sharing in community with you has been one of my greatest joys.

To my mom, who read each draft and offered helpful insights, whose enthusiasm for this project uplifted me, who babysat my kids and kept my tea supply stocked while I focused on writing: thank you for all of this and everything else. Thank you for modeling for me the joy of pursuing God; for passing on to me, and nurturing, a questing nature; and for leading the way to the church. Dad—thank you for being a constant support and a challenging interlocutor. Your commitment to tradition has been the ground of my own, and my passion for justice and zest for life come from you, too. Perhaps this book can be read in one sense as an effort to reconcile the influences of you both, and I am grateful.

To Mommom and Poppa: thank you for the Wednesday night tea times during my Fellowship. Those evenings spent sipping tea and chatting with you were a source of energy and rest, and I am grateful, as always, for your wisdom and love. Grandmom—thank you for embodying faithfulness, and for all the prayers you've offered on my behalf. And to the rest of my family, from my earliest companions to those who have come along more recently: thank you for being my people.

Shannon, Aimee, Alex, and Jen: I am grateful for your willingness to read drafts or listen to me ramble until my thoughts took some coherent shape; thank you for sharing your wisdom and friendship and the joys and struggles of motherhood.

To my St. Timothy parish family: thank you for buoying my faith and keeping me from disillusionment.

To my kids, Elena, Caleb, and Erin: thank you for being flexible and encouraging when my writing took me away from home. Thank you for being willing to share me so that I could share my own gifts; I will try to reciprocate just as selflessly as you grow up and it becomes your turn. Thank you for showing me what it means to love, and for reminding me that the world is full of hope.

And finally, to my husband, Dan, who decreased his external work hours and took on the homeschooling duties without hesitation so that I could take on the full-time work of writing: without your partnership, this book would still be a nebulous concept, and life in general would not be nearly as rich. Thank you for reading my drafts and listening to me work out ideas; for keeping our house full of laughter and good food; for always extending patience and encouragement. Thank you for all you are and all you do for our family—the journey is sweeter because we walk together.

To those mentioned here, and to all the others I have encountered along the way; to those who have come before me and cleared a path; to all who will come after me and continue the adventure: I am profoundly grateful.

Introduction

"What do I love when I love my God?"

AT ITS HEART, THIS book is an invitation to explore new dimensions of the age-old question articulated so honestly by Saint Augustine in his *Confessions*: "What do I love when I love my God?"[1] Though the answer may be elusive, the search itself holds meaning.

Recently, this question took on a new urgency for me when a loved one struggling through a mental health crisis became convinced that God was demanding retribution to punish her for her sins—after all, she said, even the New Testament is full of people enduring the justice of God's wrath. As I tried to offer support, I was forced to evaluate how well my perception of God was able to refute her tormented logic. *That is not the God I believe in* was a common and emphatic refrain of my responses. But this begged the question: what or who *is* the God I believe in?

My sense is that the church in the United States is experiencing a similar crisis of consciousness as we grapple with what it means, really, to observe the Greatest Commandment—to love God with everything in us, and to love our neighbors as ourselves. Because of the mediation of the Incarnate Christ, the Catholic tradition rejects the total, dualistic separation of divine and earthly matters. But still, it assumes "vertical" and "horizontal" dimensions of faith—vertical being that which pertains to divine matters and the soul; horizontal being that which pertains to earthly life and the body.[2] Maintaining these two dimensions functionally promotes a dualistic spirituality: if pressed, the vertical dimension always rules the horizontal. Though certainly we can say that the two are related—love of God

---

1. Augustine, *Confessions*, X.8. Unless otherwise noted, all references to this text will come from the Pine-Coffin translation.

2. See Congregation for the Doctrine of Faith, "Letter to the Bishops."

necessitates love of self and neighbor, and so on—our faith as it is currently articulated prioritizes divine reality and reinforces a hierarchical paradigm.

We speak, for example, of the clerical hierarchy, the hierarchy of truths, and a hierarchy of goods. And this paradigm resonates with our human superiority complex—the *libido dominandi*, or "lust for domination," as Augustine would say. If there is a hierarchy, we humans want to be at the top. As much as we might want to attenuate the dominative implications of hierarchical order by insisting on concepts such as servant-leadership, or the unity of body and soul, the language of hierarchy undermines these efforts.

Personally, I felt this tension during my loved one's mental health crisis: is God a kingly figure, an authoritarian doling out punishments, ruling over this world from his throne in another? And I feel it every time some well-meaning person tells me that as a Catholic mother, my primary duty is to raise my babies for heaven, as though earthly experience is only a secondary reality. We also see the problematic implications of hierarchy in the clericalism that has been under a spotlight in recent years, as well as the political posturing that conflates our political leanings with our eternal destination; or, alternatively, separates faith from the domain of politics—as though revering Christ in the Eucharist supersedes, or is even possible apart from, recognizing Christ in our marginalized neighbors, with whom Christ identifies. So what do I love when I love my God? The way we conceptualize God, and love of God, directs our activity, so our answer to the question will have profound implications.

"Beauty at once so ancient and so new" is Augustine's exquisite answer;[3] and it is there that I want to begin. What might it look like to believe in a God who is both the ground of being and yet emerges in new ways, drawing us toward the future? Is it possible to maintain our hope in the transcendent without subordinating our earthly existence? Can we eliminate dualism and hierarchy without undermining our tradition?

I think we can—if we remain open to the transformative grace of conversion.

WHY CONVERSION?

If human beings are motivated by the *libido dominandi*—if we seek domination and control—it is because we are uncomfortable with mystery. We want answers, and so we tend to stop searching when we find one that rings true—or we impose our limited sensibilities onto the unknown as though

3. Augustine, *Confessions*, X.27.

they are absolute. Indeed, I suspect that the division, hostility, and violence that mark our church and our world today are rooted in competing conceptions of who we think God is, combined with rigid confidence that what we have understood of divine matters is in fact the final word.

But beauty surprises us. It captures our attention and shakes us out of boredom, disillusionment, and intransigent self-righteousness. To experience beauty is to receive the grace that expands our horizons and invites us to move beyond ourselves, into vulnerable relationship.

Indeed, it is the poet's attention to beauty that cloaks mundane things with the aura of mystery and uncovers the delightful uncertainties that punctuate even our most emphatic convictions with question marks. Most of us too often resist this gift, planting our feet firmly on whatever solid ground we can find to carry us through this life. If instead we can open ourselves to those liminal spaces in our hearts that are not marked by assurances but by possibility, it is there that we will encounter the peace that transcends understanding.[4]

Attending to those liminal spaces requires us to be vulnerable to the disruptive turning from what we take as certain toward the unfathomable mystery, that wholeness of being that we might call God. Somewhat paradoxically, then, we must be reluctant to ascribe finality to any apprehension of the divine if we are to seek God: we must be open, always, to the grace of conversion. Conversion, though, never directs our attention toward something entirely new; rather, it reveals a way to return to our deepest longings, to those latent truths that, once acknowledged, move us beyond the limits of our current convictions.

For those of us who still attend Mass or profess our beliefs with certainty on a regular basis, the suggestion that ambiguity is grace-filled might seem suspect, and the language of conversion irrelevant. After all, our creed grounds us firmly in the truth of our faith and links us to our fellow travelers in this earthly pilgrimage. There is comfort in this. There is something reassuring about being able to point to a clearly articulated doctrinal claim to say, *That, there: that is True.* Organizing our lives in faith around these certainties calms our existential fears and allows us to act in an ordered—controllable—way.

Perhaps our reluctance to sit with the unknown stems from our desire to "be perfect" as God is perfect. After all, Jesus did exhort us to achieve this impossibility.[5] Indeed, the word used for "perfect" (τέλειος) in Matthew 5 connotes a sense of being finished, whole, and complete; of possessing ideal

4. Phil 4:7.
5. Matt 5:48.

integrity and virtue. Though we might know that our human nature prevents us, personally, from achieving such perfection, at least we belong to a church that assures us that grace covers our flaws—a church whose doctrine is complete and offers us fullness of truth, whose teachings lead us to integrity and virtue through the grace of Christ.

And yet—a crucial aspect of the truth of our reality is known through Jesus's prayer: that all "may be one, as we are one, I in them and you in me, that they may be brought to perfection as one."[6] Truth, then, cannot be known in isolation; rather, reality is constituted by relationship. The prayer of Jesus reminds us that we are brought to perfection only with those who journey with us, in unity and love.

It is interesting that the word "perfection" in John has the same root (τελ-) as that used in Matthew 5, above, as though to indicate that we are never "complete" apart from our relationships with our companions in the community of being: we are finished, brought to completion, and made virtuous only through relationships. And relationships are messy, nuanced, and intuitive; they must be worked out with vulnerability and uncertainty through embodied, practical, responsive engagement.

Thus, if faith and reason are the two wings "on which the human spirit rises to the contemplation of truth,"[7] relationships constitute the very air that enables flight. As Ilia Delio puts it, our faith "calls us to recognize that connectedness is a basic reality of our existence."[8] Indeed, we know now that a worldview premised on a static order of hierarchy fails to provide a paradigm sufficient for understanding our reality. The cosmos is not ordered by hierarchy, but by interconnection, and it is dynamic—ever-expanding and evolving, always becoming more whole.

Since every part of creation "tells the glory of God,"[9] every being has something to teach us about who God is. From the beginning of time, creation has been energized to develop more diverse forms of being and to form increasingly complex relationships through enfolding what exists into the emergence of new entities. And as contemporary scientific insights reveal, we humans are quite literally interconnected with one another and our planet—my being is tied to yours, as well as that of the stars and the sea, and each of us is part of the creation story.

This awareness should draw us beyond ourselves in recognition that our perceptions are, as Christopher Pramuk has put it, "partial and

6. John 17:21–23.

7. John Paul II, *Fides et Ratio*, Preface.

8. Delio, *Making All Things New*, 199.

9. Ps 19:1.

contingent to the one great fellowship and gift in which we all—inclusive of the natural world—live, move, and have our being."[10] We are never justified in complacency, in believing ourselves to have attained truth in its entirety and thus to have reached the end of our search for God. To seek truth is to embrace mystery, and this requires continuous conversion as we loosen our grip on our most guarded ideals and allow the Spirit to expand the horizons of our perception through new relationships. In this way, rather than rising to contemplate truth, we have to travel on the ground, through the mud, always open to traversing boundaries and following new paths. "I am part of a whole, like you," Delio reminds us, "and the whole is more than any one of us can grasp because the absolute wholeness of life is love itself—God—the power of the future."[11]

Without openness to new encounters, experiences, or ways of thinking, theology becomes unwieldy and oppressive, and the tradition that should serve to ground the church and nurture its engagement with the world can serve instead to choke the life out of spiritual growth. When we stop searching, we become stagnant, unwilling to acknowledge that there may be revelation that we previously failed to recognize or understand, or new ways to interpret what has been revealed.

Realizing that God is wholly present but not wholly knowable in every bit of matter and energy should open us to the possibility that we draw closer to God through encounter with the ones in whom God is present, and that whatever we think we know about God is only a fraction of the ultimate wholeness of love that is the source and empowerment of all being. Indeed, if we know anything about God, we know that the Spirit that was present at the creation of the world is one of action: the Spirit *moves*—drawing what is into what could be. And we know now that interconnectedness is not just a spiritual reality, but an empirical one, as well: we see this reflected in all of creation, which is always developing toward ever greater consciousness and new relationships.

But though we are evolving, we do not evolve from nothing: the tradition through which we express our hope undergirds any progress we might make. As Delio puts it, "Religion is not something one arrives at; rather, it is the starting point for relationship with the absolute one—God."[12] The tradition that grounds our faith should be enfolded and enlivened through the emergence of new relationships—beauty ever ancient *and* ever new.

---

10. Pramuk, *Hope Sings,* 23.
11. Delio, *Making All Things New,* 199.
12. Delio, *Making All Things New,* 196.

To be perfect, then, we Catholics must be about "becoming one"— with emphasis on becoming. For us, there is no fixed end point for unity, and we cannot hope to apprehend the fullness of truth—the great mystery that is God—apart from the relationships that constitute the reality of our existence. We always can expand our horizons through encountering and engaging with others and the world, and these encounters should motivate conversion as we apprehend a fuller reality and allow ourselves to be transformed. Though we often think of the word "Catholic" as meaning "universal," a better understanding connotes wholeness. As Delio has pointed out, Catholicity is "an orientation toward the whole by one who has a sense of the whole."[13] God, the love that creates and sustains the world, is found in and with and through the many who, together, evolve toward oneness.

PLAN

When I reflect on my own spiritual journey, I can point to particular encounters that shaped my understanding of God by opening me up to new, shared horizons. Though I recognize them as grace-filled and pregnant with transcendent meaning, these encounters inevitably brought me out of the world of abstractions, directing my moral vision outward in relationships. In what follows, I recount these experiences with hope that my reflections offer an opportunity for you, reader, to enter into those liminal spaces in your own heart.

When I first encountered Saint Augustine through reading his *Confessions* in college, I was enthralled. I saw myself mirrored in his relentless pursuit of truth, as well as his ambition, passion, and orientation toward justice. He has been a companion on my journey ever since. What holds my attention, I think, is Augustine's persistence in his striving. Not content to become complacent, or to claim to have understood God, Augustine keeps up the search. And as he struggles to make sense of his past errors, he recognizes the grace that was present within them, and which has drawn him beyond.

In chapter 1, then, I will explore the various contours of Augustine's thought that have been most meaningful to me. I engage with him here to explore how this encounter inspired my initial conversion to the Catholic Church, and to interrogate the evolution of my own theological framework.

"You have made us for yourself, and our hearts are restless until they rest in you."[14] Has there ever been a more poignant expression to capture the

13. Delio, *Making All Things New*, 35.
14. Augustine, *Confessions*, I.1.

spark of human existence? This phrase, one of Augustine's most recognized, contains within it the crux of Augustinian theology that captured my imagination: human beings have a purpose—individually and collectively—and we are dissatisfied and unstable until we embody it. For Augustine, of course, the purpose of human beings is to rest in God, for God is the ultimate good toward which all other goods—and all our striving—are oriented.

Writing at the turn of the fifth century, Augustine maintains the hierarchical cosmology of the ancients: there is, he thinks, a hierarchy of being, characterized by the superiority of eternal, spiritual goods over temporal and physical ones—although, as will become clear, this paradigm is tempered by his embrace of the biblical cosmology of the goodness of creation and the incarnation of Christ.[15] On his account, human beings occupy the highest place in the hierarchy of physical beings and are able to traverse the gap between earthly and divine spheres thanks to our intellects and the mediation of Christ. Augustine builds on this idea to develop an account of the *ordo amoris*, or order of love, through which the soul can ascend to God.

We see here an early articulation of the division between vertical and horizontal dimensions of faith, which I wish to bring together. But it is a gift of Augustine's thought that despite the constraints his hierarchical paradigm placed on his own theology, he nevertheless developed tools to help us to sift through the false binaries that the language of hierarchy promotes: soul *or* body; traditional *or* progressive; piety *or* justice; vertical *or* horizontal. Exploring the order of love in light of the knowledge we have gained over the past 1,500 years can help illuminate the beauty of Augustine's account, as well as its pitfalls.

While it was Augustine's influence that first drew me to the Catholic Church, my engagement with women religious in the work for peace and justice drew me more deeply into Catholic faith. Between 2017 and 2021, I worked with Dianna Ortiz, OSU, of the Center of Concern's Education for Justice Project, and I served with the School Sisters of Notre Dame, Atlantic-Midwest Province, in the Office of Justice, Peace, and Integrity of Creation, where I was assistant director to Arlene Flaherty, a Dominican Sister. These women of faith introduced me to new ways of being Catholic by humbly and prophetically living in right relationships within community. They expressed spiritual sensibilities that emphasized encounter and inclusion: their love was ordered, in practice, toward relationship before dogma. Through them, I learned to define Catholicism in terms of wholeness and interconnection, rather than hierarchy.

15. See Ogle, *Politics and the Earthly City*, 134.

Chapter 2, then, illuminates this second conversion. Through exploring the relationships I formed with these women of the church, I reflect on the subtle differences between their way of being Catholic and mine, and I unpack how I became aware of the problematic implications of the hierarchical worldview that orders the church and Western society. In the process, I critique Augustine's faulty cosmology of hierarchy, which has been handed down through church structures and doctrinal interpretations and has lent itself to discord rather than unity by playing into the human lust for domination.

Indeed, if the *libido dominandi* is a root of sin, it is not surprising that a theology built around hierarchy has lent itself to the implementation of oppressive structures in the church and in Western society, generally. We cannot expect our doctrinal interpretations to reflect the reality of our interconnected existence if our mode of theological discernment has been exclusionary. Thus, it is important to grapple with the implications of theological doctrines developed and controlled by an all-male, primarily white and Western, hierarchy. My experience with the SSND is a helpful starting point for this discussion, since they trace their spiritual heritage to Augustine and embody the charism of unity, directing their "entire lives toward that oneness for which Jesus Christ was sent."[16]

Chapter 3 articulates the cosmological consciousness being developed and nurtured within communities of women religious, as they seek God—the wholeness of being—through and with, rather than "above," matter. Here, I will explore how new cosmology resonates with my Augustinian spirituality and the connective threads I find between the two. The import of cosmological spirituality lies not only in its empirical and intuitive accuracy, I argue, but also—and primarily—in the way it generates openness to imaginative horizons, resists stagnancy, and merges the vertical and horizontal dimensions of faith.

Chapter 4 considers how new cosmology can enrich our faith tradition by exploring the doctrines of original sin and the grace of Christ through its lens. Although the term "cosmology" might raise concerns in some readers, even among women religious,[17] the term simply refers to the science of the universe, and the metaphysical implications of its origins and development. To speak of a cosmological spirituality, then, is to recognize that the order and workings of the universe can teach us about God and ourselves. Augustine's cosmology was one of hierarchy, which led to a distorted sense of

16. School Sisters of Notre Dame, *You Are Sent*, I.4.

17. For a rich exploration of the different approaches and responses to new cosmology among women religious, see Brink, *Heavens Are Telling*.

order; the cosmological spirituality awakening in many women religious is one of interconnection, which appears to be more spiritually and empirically sound. By gesturing toward some doctrinal implications, this chapter opens up the imaginative space to reflect on tradition in new light.

I should note at the outset that while what we know of the universe story offers insights into our human story, as well, the spirituality being developed here does not depend on getting that story entirely right. In other words, I do not mean to suggest that what we have learned about the cosmos is itself absolute. Rather, the call to be open to evolution and expansion—the call to seek unity through encounter—is also a spiritual one that seems to be reflected in our natural world. The way the natural world adheres to this call is instructive, but not decisive, and if future data leads us to recast our cosmological hypotheses, then we can do so in light of our call to oneness. We humans have to devise the best interpretations of our reality based on the information available to us—but we always must remain open to adjusting to new insights. The cosmological framework offered here can teach us how to do so.

Chapter 5 reflects on the significance of this cosmological spirituality for life today. My work for peace and justice is rooted in Augustine's influence, but during the turmoil of the past few years—from existential threats to political violence to racial reckoning—even his theology of rightly ordered love and right relationships seemed to reinforce my *libido dominandi*, my desire for control, as I clung vehemently to my own sense of "right." I find it difficult to imagine what unity could even look like in such times. But embracing cosmic consciousness allows for creativity—for our limits and vulnerabilities to inspire new relationships and ways of being in the world. Exploring ways in which the SSND and other women religious embody this consciousness will bring to life its import.

The response of the Leadership Conference of Women Religious (LCWR) during the Vatican investigation of their activity from 2009–2015 offers a particularly compelling example of choosing love and humility over power or domination. In the face of humiliation and derision, they maintained a posture of reconciliation, rather than self-righteousness. Reflecting on their ordeal and the theological framework that guided them through it provides a helpful way to imagine what it might mean to embody the integrity of conviction, even as we remain open to change. In the activities of these women religious, we see an expression of love ordered toward wholeness rather than *right*.

Through my work with the SSND, I came to realize that an order that reinforces hierarchy is inherently false—it cannot be the right order of love. Truth, instead, is found through the messy uncertainty that comes from opening ourselves to love. Augustine tells us that "falsehood consists in not living in the way for which [we were] created,"[18] so if the cosmos is evolutive and interrelational, then truth inheres in evolutive and expansive relationship with our neighbors in the community of being, as we become ever more conscious of the whole toward which we are evolving.

But what does it mean to seek God as the wholeness of being and to order our loves accordingly? Chapter 6 explores an answer that emerges from Augustine's account of the soul's ascent to God. In the face of existential crises and the hostility and division that mark our lives today, this Augustinian framework, illuminated by the spirituality of women religious, can contribute to the mission of "making one" and can help to foster unity and wholeness within the church and throughout the world. I make this case by reframing Augustine's concept of love from one that ascends in truth to one that expands in encounter.

By eliminating the hierarchical tendencies of Augustine's worldview, we can flip the *ordo amoris* horizontally, as it were, and reorient our pursuit of truth outward through encounter rather than upward toward a fixed essence. In doing so, we can maintain a theological posture that is relational, rather than legalistic; creatively evolutive while grounded in tradition; and humble, without being relativistic. By reorienting the horizons of our love toward the whole, we can keep Augustine's idea of ordered "ascent" but turn it over into a concept of inclusive expansion. And this entails, especially, encountering those on the margins.

Imagining the Catholic faith tradition through the lens of this Augustinian framework, informed by the witness of women religious and the marginalized members of our community of being, can help to ground our theology in the material and yet meet our yearning for the transcendent. By merging our sense of the divine with the whole toward which we are evolving, we can embrace the whole of ourselves in our physical reality, living in communion with others and sharing our gifts with this world. Ronald Rolheiser, OMI, puts it powerfully: "The earth is ablaze with the fire of God. . . . The fire, the relentless pressure, is not only in the soul; it is in everything else as well. The cosmos is all of a piece. The chemicals in your hand and in your brain were forged by the same furnace, the furnace of the stars. The story of life, body, and soul is written in DNA—and relentless yearning lies just as much in the cosmos and the DNA as it lies in our hearts and souls."[19] Directing our vision toward the whole can help us refocus away from esoteric or

---

18. Augustine, *City of God*, XIV.4.
19. Rolheiser, *Against an Infinite Horizon*, 15.

other-worldly concerns and connect to God at the heart of matter as we root ourselves in transcendent love.

Today's fractured world is desperately in need of Catholics willing to be authentic whole-makers, to "be conscious that each life breath that I call my own belongs to the stars, the galaxies, my neighbors and family, my enemies, past generations, and those to come."[20] Through understanding God as the energy that links us to the past, emerges in new ways in the present, and draws us toward a future of wholeness, the church can carry out its sacramental mission of unity more fully by adjusting its reliance on hierarchical order toward an embrace of enfolded, interrelational order; adopting humility as the key to actualizing Christ's love in the world; and reimagining faith in a way that merges vertical and horizontal dimensions.

At the same time, this interrelational sense of order should offer evaluative tools for assessing the validity of our interpretations—we can evaluate what is emerging by considering the way in which it enfolds the tradition that birthed it, as well as how it furthers the call to oneness. In other words, though new interpretations might diverge from previously held conceptions as new perspectives are invited into the discussion, there should be continuity with those aspects of the faith tradition that, themselves, are ordered toward expansive encounter. Indeed, an evolving consciousness is a sign of the Spirit at work.

By highlighting this enfolded order, I hope to bridge the dualistic gap between tradition and progress, and to invite readers toward a deeper consciousness of the wholeness of being, the unity of God.

EVER ANCIENT, EVER NEW

For context, Saint Augustine's world, like ours, was full of turbulence. He lived during the fall of the Roman Empire. He died as his city of Hippo was under siege by Vandals from the north, who had invaded Africa and ravaged the cities along their path. In between, he had consequential theological disagreements with the Manicheans, who embraced dualism; Pelagians, who maintained that human effort alone was sufficient for goodness; and Donatists, fundamentalists who insisted that the purity of the church should be absolute if sacraments were to be valid. These theological disagreements also played out in the political realm, and Augustine used his influence to advocate for justice for the marginalized: criminals and their families, refugees, human trafficking victims, and the materially poor, among others.

20. Delio, *Making All Things New*, 199.

I see parallels of his situation in our time, as well: we, too, are experiencing a massive cultural upheaval that feels like the death throes of an empire—or perhaps the birth pangs of a new era. We, too, have deep philosophical and moral disagreements that set us against each other, and it seems impossible to compromise without capitulating to "the enemy"—indeed, it is easy to spot contemporary iterations of each of Augustine's primary theological opponents. The polarization and partisanship in the United States has reached record levels, and confined to echo chambers and virtual realities, we have closed in on ourselves with individualistic worldviews—worldviews that cannot reflect the truth of our existence.

The Spirit, however, moves toward unity. While the falsehood of division is evident as much in the church as in the public square, the creative love of God moves toward ever expansive connections and greater consciousness. In this, there is hope.

As we analyze the signs of the times, this framework of encounter that brings together the old and the new into a holistic worldview can offer a helpful way of thinking about what it means to relate rightly to God, others, and ourselves. I write these reflections not because I think I have arrived at truth or perfection, but because I know we cannot search for them alone. If we are open to the movement of the Spirit and the grace of conversion, the relational contours of our faith will help us to bear witness to the love that draws us beyond ourselves, toward wholeness of being.

The purpose of this book, then, is to contribute to the development of a theology that reflects the evolutive force of relationship: a theology that is rooted in tradition, responsive to present realities, and ever open to the future—a theology that situates faith and reason within the context of encounter.

So, the question remains: what do we love when we love our God? Following the wisdom of the poet, let us look, and laugh in astonishment, and bow our heads.[21]

21. Oliver, "Mysteries, Yes," in Oliver, *Evidence*, 62.

1

Seeking Truth with Saint Augustine

An Intellectual Conversion

I am grateful to have been loved and to be loved now and to be able to love, because that liberates. Love liberates. It doesn't just hold— that's ego. Love liberates.

—MAYA ANGELOU

SOMETIMES, WE EXPERIENCE AN event and immediately know it will be transformative; more often, the moments that define our lives seem insignificant, receding into the labyrinth of memory to influence our consciousness in subtle yet insistent ways. In his *Confessions*, Augustine invites us to explore with him "the more obscure depths of the *memoria*" and probes his consciousness to discover the hints of truth buried along the path of his life's journey—he seeks "to disclose to the mind's conscious gaze the truth lying latent and unsuspected within itself."[1] Though few of us, perhaps, may be gifted with Augustine's introspective acuity, each of us can benefit from such an exploratory exercise. For self-knowledge, to borrow from Ian

---

1. Markus, "Augustine. Reason and Illumination," in Armstrong, *Cambridge History*, 372. See Augustine, *On the Trinity*, XV.21.40.

Clausen, "is not an end in itself but unfolds in the infinite mystery and otherness of God."[2]

When I was nine years old, I went for a walk with my family. A recent rainstorm had caused the surrounding area to become saturated with water, and runoff trickled down our street toward the sewer. Curious, we began to follow the path of the water—stepping off the street to walk beside the spill stream that fed the runoff, and traipsing through the woods to discover the increasingly larger streams that had spilled over, pouring out in rivulets. Having continuously surpassed its boundaries and made new paths, the water invited us to do the same. Though I was ill-prepared for such a muddy adventure, wearing regular sneakers instead of rain boots, I was delighted to see my footprints tracking alongside a fawn's as we pressed further through the wild, toward the elusive source of the overflow.

After calling an end to the search, we went home and got cleaned up, and I relegated this experience to the category of pleasant memories. But a newly awakened desire to find the source of things—and delight in the challenge of the pursuit—has informed my identity ever since.

Augustine identifies the source of things as God: the One who Is, the whole, eternal truth; and he proposes that delight in truth is the defining experience of Christian faith—indeed, it is the purpose for which human beings were made. "You made us with yourself as our goal," he writes, "and our heart is restless until it rests in you."[3] The human heart searches persistently for anything that can hold the expanse of its love; it succeeds, Augustine tells us, by holding fast to eternal truth.

It was, in fact, the Catholic tradition's emphasis on truth, and its insistence upon the compatibility of faith and reason, delight and intellectual rigor, that captured my religious imagination and drew me into its fold. I was raised as an Evangelical Protestant, where my religious sensibilities were formed with an emphasis on emotional responses and metaphysical realities, often at the expense of practical wisdom. I grew up believing that Jesus Christ came to this earth from his supernatural kingdom to save sinners from hell, and it was my responsibility to make sure everyone knew it. I can remember asking strangers if they had "accepted Jesus into their heart," and my loftiest goal as a kid was to be a missionary to a foreign nation—to "win souls for Christ." This, I did out of love for God and neighbor—and perhaps, slightly, a selfish desire for approval.

Mine was a tight-knit faith community. All of my best friends and mentors attended the same church, so I associated faith with friendship,

2. Clausen, *On Love*, 126.
3. Augustine, *Confessions*, I.1, trans. Ruden.

and devotion to God was as much a spiritual exercise as an expression of social pressure. The Bible served as history and science textbook, and I had read it through by my tenth birthday.

I can remember a Sunday school lesson entitled, "Why Should I Believe the Bible?" It enumerated a list of reasons, including 1) "It is the Word of God"; and 2) "It was written by many human authors over thousands of years and yet it never contradicts itself." At the time, I did not have the intellectual tools to identify the first as circular reasoning, but I did wrestle with the second claim. Realizing that the first two chapters of Genesis contain two different accounts of creation, I simply could not accept this principle of non-contradiction at face value. Rather than reaffirm my belief in the Bible's literal veracity—which I actually had never questioned—it changed the trajectory of my Christian life. In that moment, though I was not fully aware of its significance at the time, I began to hunger for an intellectually satisfying faith.

I see now that by acknowledging an area of lack, I could make room for sustenance; by questioning my conception of the absolute, I could lean into the challenge and uncertainty of spiritual pursuit. Although I am embarrassed to recall some aspects of my Evangelical upbringing, the truth is that the sense of belonging I experienced in this faith community inspired the joy I find in the pursuit of God, and the formation I received there expanded my moral vision outward in love and care for the wellbeing of strangers, though my definition of love has evolved. Like water that spills over and over into ever new places, God is not confined to one tributary. I have carried this awareness ever since. To seek the source, I have come to realize, we must continually expand the parameters of our search.

In his *Confessions*, Augustine experiences a similar epiphany. Augustine spends nine years as a practicing member of a religion known as Manicheism, but suddenly he becomes aware that some of the teachings of his faith are empirically disprovable: the Manichean books, he writes, contain obvious "false statements about the sky and the stars and the movements of the sun and moon."[4] He abandons the desire to become a full-fledged member of the Manichean sect once he becomes aware that Mani, its founder, "spoke not only ignorantly but even deceptively, and with psychotic self-regard."[5] Even the great Manichean orator, Faustus, Augustine recognizes as "quite uninformed."[6] In light of these realizations, Augustine determines that whatever else faith entails, it should not demand the explicit

4. Augustine, *Confessions*, V.8, trans. Ruden.
5. Augustine, *Confessions*, V.8, trans. Ruden.
6. Augustine, *Confessions*, V.7.

rejection or suppression of rational knowledge. Still, he "did not cut himself off entirely from the Manichees," at this point, but "decided to be content with [the beliefs] for the time being, unless something preferable clearly presented itself."[7]

Truth is attractive. As human beings with the capacity for reason, we are drawn to rational claims. Indeed, for Augustine, the intellect is one of the most important aspects of human personhood, and it is critical for knowing God. The intellect can grasp the concept of an infinite good, the One who Is,[8] through the "never changing, true eternity of truth,"[9] Augustine writes. Truth, he tells us, is constant and unchanging—"the same yesterday, and today, and forever."[10] We humans, trying to make sense of our capricious desires and the whims of fate, feel at peace when we cling "to this firm rock of truth."[11]

Importantly, though, the intellect is not the only aspect of our humanity, and Augustine recognizes that it is love that moves us toward truth and inspires us to remain in its light. It is also love that leads us astray and entices us to be deceived.

TRUTH'S ORDER

For Augustine, the world exists in this interplay of truth and love, and the One creates and sustains a world ordered toward wholeness. As Joseph Torchia observes, "In Augustinian terms, the universe is a 'cosmos' in the classical sense of that term—that is, an ordered scheme whose parts share in and derive their intelligibility from the greater whole."[12] This order is characterized by a hierarchy of being, in which the "higher things are better than the lower, [though] the sum of all creation is better than the higher things alone."[13] All that exists receives its being from the One who Is—from goodness, truth, and being itself.[14] Therefore, Augustine concludes, "whatever is, is good," although, he submits, all things are not equally good.[15]

---

7. Augustine, *Confessions*, V.7.

8. Augustine, *Confessions*, VII.17.

9. Augustine, *Confessions*, VII.17.

10. Heb 13:8.

11. Augustine, *Confessions*, IV.14.

12. Torchia, "Significance of *Ordo*," in Lienhard et al., *Augustine*, 270.

13. Augustine, *Confessions*, VII.13.

14. Augustine, *Confessions*, VII.10.

15. Augustine, *Confessions*, VII.12.

Because he maintains a biblical vision of created goodness, Augustine avoids the worst of the dualism that could attend this hierarchical model. Veronica Ogle, for example, recognizes that for Augustine, "the incarnation reveals that the only significant criterion for superiority is nearness to God,"[16] though nearness to God is attained by identifying with the humble Christ and ascending through vertical tiers of being.

In this hierarchy of being, humans occupy the highest tier available to material beings, followed by animals, plants, and inanimate objects. Augustine recognizes that the goodness of all things is both a gift and a source of temptation: when we are deluded into loving "lower" things more than "higher," we become weighted down and are inhibited from making our ascent to truth; but still, we can "catch sight of the truth as he is known through his creation."[17] According to Augustine, when we recognize the truth in this hierarchy we will so delight in it that we will align our priorities to act according to the order inherent in it. When we disrupt or ignore the order, our restless hearts feel the tension.

Augustine tells us that "the peace of all things is a tranquillity of order [sic]. Order is the classification of things equal and unequal that assigns to each its proper position."[18] When we delight in the truth, then, we act in ways that promote the full participation of every being in the cosmos, according to the kind of being it is and its place in the hierarchy. Truth assures us that every being matters, and that the whole is greater than the sum of the parts; though some parts, for Augustine, matter less than others.

The ethic that emerges from Augustine is one of ordered priorities within relationships, and it is intuitively satisfying, I think. We have to have some way to sort through all the moral claims imposed on us in virtue of our humanity, and it will not due to dispense with notions of natural order insofar as we act reflexively according to a paradigm of hierarchy. For example, whether I am aware of it or not, my sense of the order of being will determine my response to the following questions: Is it more important to keep my family's food fresh, or to preserve the lives of a pantry moth and its larvae? Should I walk the mile to the store or drive my gas-powered minivan? Should we impose restrictions on activity to limit the spread of a potentially deadly virus, or should we keep everything up and running to ensure economic stability? In other words—what do, or should, I love more? Considering each good according to the order of being can help us make the difficult choices. But what happens when we get the order wrong?

16. Ogle, *Politics and the Earthly City*, 134.

17. Augustine, *Confessions*, VII.10.

18. Augustine, *City of God*, XIX.13.

PARTIAL KNOWLEDGE

When we take our own partial understanding of the good and assign to it an absolute value that it does not possess, we exceed our limits. And the human lust for domination—the striving to exceed our limits—is precisely where Augustine locates sin.

For him, truth compels us to relate rightly to others, but when the truth in which we delight is misconstrued or underdeveloped, our activity will be misdirected, too. It can be quite dangerous if we conflate our sense of the eternal law with absolute moral requirements in earthly endeavors.

Looking back at my childhood, for example, I remember laughing smugly with a friend in civics class about the hypocrisy of our liberal peers: *their slogan should be save the trees; kill the babies*, I quipped. And I am deeply ashamed to confess that I simply nodded when a friend implied that only those Black people who embodied white culture were worthy of our friendship. It never struck me as problematic that there were few people of color present in my classes, nor did I lose sleep over the fact that I befriended few of the Hispanic students who attended our school, though I took advantage of the labor of many of their families, who supplied my rural community with the fresh produce that nourished our bodies and fed our identity. I did, however, march against abortion rights and invite people to church.

Still, as I recall, I embodied a strong sense of justice and was always ready to stand with those I perceived to be marginalized—like my grandmother, who worked as a nurse in underprivileged communities because, she said, *those of us with privilege can get care whenever we need it; who will give the poor the care they deserve?* The problem, I see now, is that my perception of who was actually vulnerable, or the ways actions and policies affected them, was skewed. I had not yet acknowledged the lack in my moral judgment.

It is a feature of the human condition that we want to believe ourselves to be right and whole, and a tragic irony that our understanding always must be limited and partial. This is why Augustine holds relationality and humility to be the keys to truth-seeking and just activity. As Torchia writes, "Augustine links his understanding of iniquity as the will's aversion from 'what is Divine and abiding' with the 'whole'/'part' analysis that we encounter throughout his moral deliberations. . . . Sin is viewed as a rejection of the universal good in favor of limited, partial goods proper to oneself alone."[19]

Often, I think, we try to ameliorate this disconcerting tension by imagining "vertical" and "horizontal" dimensions of faith. In the hierarchy of

19. Torchia, "The Significance of *Ordo*," in Lienhard et al., *Augustine*, 269.

truth, the vertical dimensions—those elements of faith related to eternal matters of the soul—are most important, though in their fullness, they certainly motivate love of neighbor in the horizontal plane and serve to bring others to salvation. The horizontal goods are always defined and constrained by the vertical, eternal, order of truth.

But if Augustine is right, and human habits keep us from choosing the good by turning us inward and keeping us focused only on what we think is good *for us*, we must grapple with the possibility that our preconceived or traditional "vertical" ideals might be distorted, limited, or otherwise blurry. Like Saint Paul's looking glass, our individual perspectives obscure important features of truth.[20]

This is not only a personal issue: distorted ideals can become normalized in social life and often are reflected by and perpetuated through oppressive social structures. In Augustine's words, "We are carried away by custom to our own undoing and it is hard to struggle against the stream."[21]

Of course, I was blissfully unaware of these dangers for most of my life. I had no grasp, for example, of the systemic blockades that deter many students of color from being placed in upper-level academic tracks, or the problematic implications of associating normalcy with white cultural preferences. I did not see the hypocrisy of celebrating the bountiful harvest at the county festival each October, while encouraging systemic measures to marginalize, traumatize, or endanger those whose labor supplied the fruit. I was convinced that climate change was a concern contrived by tree-hugging fanatics looking for a reason to be angry. And poverty, of course, I recognized as a state brought on by an individual's lack of effort since in America, we can pull ourselves up by our bootstraps.[22]

I see now that these convictions share in common a dependence upon an order of being that asserts the superiority of white humans. Identifying God with truth, and truth with its white, Western face distorted my apprehension of the full order of truth. When I held this order to be absolute, my moral growth was stunted.

20. 1 Cor 13:12.

21. Augustine, *Confessions*, I.16.

22. For further research on these subjects and their intersections, see Bonilla-Silva, *Racism without Racists*; and Oluo, *So You Want to Talk about Race*.

KNOWING TRUTH[23]

The turning point for me occurred inside a maximum-security prison. I had spent the first few years of college restlessly pursuing intellectual satiety—during my first and second undergraduate years, I transferred from Kutztown University, a small state school in rural Pennsylvania, to Temple University in Philadelphia, where I attended just long enough to meet the man who would become my husband, and finally to Villanova University, where I would complete my degree in philosophy. As part of my degree program there, I enrolled in a course on theology and criminal justice, which included an opportunity to volunteer as a tutor in the education department of Graterford Penitentiary, a maximum-security prison hidden in a Philadelphia suburb.

It is the smell that I remember most. Something about the staleness of the air catches in your nostrils, as though even the oxygen has been excluded from engaging with the outside world. Walking down the green linoleum hallway, casting furtive and curious glances from side to side, I felt—somewhat ashamedly—the privilege of my ability to come and go as I pleased. And from the first time I was introduced to the men in the education department, I felt their exclusion to be profoundly unjust.

I had, at the time, no real exposure to criminals or crime, but many staunchly held ideals about justice. If someone broke the law, he or she was to be held accountable, regardless of race, class, or gender. As for the accountability process itself, it had not occurred to me to question its internal justice—after all, the legal process is premised on fairness, and a convicted offender must deserve the punishment the state deems suitable. My conception of justice was grounded upon my understanding of the eternal law, which reinforced my sense of its objectivity. "Facts are stubborn things," John Adams is said to have averred, and this perception informed my political and social ideals.

All of this was turned on its head, however, the first time I personally encountered the men who were on the receiving end of the strong fist of "justice"—the first time my carefully constructed theories met with the messy reality of the lives of actual people. When the inmates primarily responsible for running the education department introduced themselves and the program, I was astonished by their kindness, humility, and intellect. The men were both "lifers"—one of them had been imprisoned since he was a

---

23. The paragraphs in this section have been adapted from Bonnette, "Branch Regrafted."

teenager for a gang-related murder—yet these were not the hate-filled good-for-nothings of my cinematic imagination.

Throughout my term as a tutor in the prison, I struggled to reconcile my ideals of justice with the reality of the offenders. I began to realize that the conclusions that we draw concerning the application of faith and morals are valid only insofar as our premises are valid. And if our premises are malformed, as when they are developed in an echo-chamber, they cannot capture the full reality of experience. My ideals were shaken from their moorings, and I knew I needed to reorganize my worldview to make sense of the experience.

CONVERSION

Soon after, I encountered Augustine in his *Confessions* and my journey took a new turn. Here was a brilliant thinker, articulating questions about God and human experience in a way that was both passionate and creative. The integration of intellect, emotion, and creativity in his theology struck me as authentically human and resonated with the pieces of myself that had been excluded from faith endeavors to that point. His relational ethic helped me to understand how to merge my belief in absolute truth with my new-found awareness that, sometimes, legalistic frameworks cannot do justice to the experience of life. In Augustine's theological approach, I found an open invitation to question, and the beauty I discovered in the depth of his intellectual search captured my own religious imagination and turned my attention toward the Catholic Church.

Augustine, too, experiences an imaginative expansion that initiates his conversion. He recalls trying to conceptualize God using a spatial framework that is not up to the task: "My wits were so blunt," he confesses, "that I thought that whatever had no dimensions in space must be absolutely nothing at all."[24] Eventually, he realizes that his unwieldy framework limits his appreciation of who God is. Reflecting on why he held obstinately to this theory of God, Augustine tells us he "could imagine [God] in no other way."[25] Reorienting his thinking opens his imaginative capacity and enables his mind to contemplate truth.

Augustine describes his conversion as beginning with a textual encounter, as well: for him, it was Cicero's *Hortensius* that "altered [his] outlook on life."[26] He recalls that upon reading Cicero's work, "All my empty dreams

24. Augustine, *Confessions*, VII.1.

25. Augustine, *Confessions*, VII.1.

26. Augustine, *Confessions*, III.4.

suddenly lost their charm and my heart began to throb with a bewildering passion for the wisdom of eternal truth. I began to climb out of the depths to which I had sunk, in order to return to you."[27] Later, after nearly a decade of false starts and misdirection, his mind rediscovers the ultimate good, eternal truth: "In an instant of awe," he writes, "my mind attained to the sight of the God who is. Then, at last, I caught sight of your invisible nature, as it is known through your creatures. But I had no strength to fix my gaze upon them. In my weakness I recoiled and fell back into my old ways, carrying with me nothing but the memory of something that I loved and longed for."[28] In this epiphany, Augustine's soul "attains to the sight of the God who is" when his intellect is illumined by the light of eternal truth.

LOVE'S KNOWING

Augustine finally makes the decision to be baptized in the Catholic Church after a period of intense internal struggle. His intellect has apprehended truth, but his will resists assenting to its demands. Augustine prayed, as my Irish Catholic grandfather likes to recall with a grin, "God, give me chastity and continence, but not yet."[29] So, Augustine wrestles with the disconnect: his soul "is wrenched in two and suffers great trials, because while truth teaches it to prefer one course, habit prevents it from relinquishing the other."[30] Eventually, he experiences an episode that reflects the emotional pull of faith as he, through his tears, hears the admonition, *tolle lege*: take it up and read. Upon indiscriminately flipping open a Bible and landing upon Saint Paul's instruction to "put on Jesus Christ,"[31] Augustine recalls that "all the darkness of doubt was dispelled."[32]

Augustine realizes that the pleasures of the flesh that had dominated his activity were enslaving him because they were not directed toward their eternal end—they were exceeding the limits of their proper order. Through his description of this conversion, Augustine illustrates the holistic way in which the intellect and will must be united through love to ascend (and assent) to God. Love is the critical feature of a person's ascent to truth since it directs the will toward that which delights it, but if it is misdirected, it

---

27. Augustine, *Confessions*, III.4.

28. Augustine, *Confessions*, VII.17.

29. Augustine, *Confessions*, VIII.7.

30. Augustine, *Confessions*, VIII.10.

31. Rom 13:14.

32. Augustine, *Confessions*, VIII.12.

turns false. Indeed, Augustine argues elsewhere that "no good is completely known which is not completely loved."[33]

Although the Catholic Church is not often perceived as a paragon of free thinking—and neither is Augustine, for that matter—this spirit of inquiry drew me to the church, and I was confirmed during the Easter Vigil of 2011. Once, during a retreat for catechumens that I attended in preparation for joining the church, I walked through a labyrinth garden, my prayers mimicking the rambling of my movement as I tried to discern whether to continue my graduate studies. Quite clearly and suddenly, the phrase "live in love, not in fear" resonated in my spirit. I understood this to be a maxim based on Scripture: "perfect love drives out fear."[34] Like the passage that inspired Augustine to live with loves ordered according to the hierarchy of truth, the exhortation to live in love, rather than fear, settled my anxious mind and offered a rubric for decision-making that has served as a guidepost ever since.

"The heart knows everything,"[35] Joy Harjo reminds us, and only through its love can that which is strange or unknown be seen clearly. Though the heart is susceptible to deception, its role in truth-seeking is critical. This is why love casts out fear: when we attend to those who are mysterious—as all others must be, on some level—the uncertainties that cause self-concern to eclipse other-regard evaporate, and exaggerated worries about potential pitfalls are attenuated. Love moves us to relate to those around us in a way that views them in the fullness of their being, through the eyes of God, who is truth, who is love.

For Augustine, love casts out fear because it prioritizes rightly. Love, when it is ordered toward truth, does not seek domination or control; love opens us to receive the gift of the other, despite the vulnerability to transformation and the inevitability of loss. When our love is ordered toward what is eternal, we can appreciate the gifts of this world authentically, as they participate in the broader whole, without fear of losing them. As Ogle observes, "Because those nearer to God yearn for others to share in their fellowship, the cosmos is revealed to be animated by an economy of gift, or service, not an economy of power."[36]

Again, it is fundamental to Augustine's thinking that everything that God creates is good (although all things are not equally good). Every creature participates in the order of the cosmos and both constitutes and is

33. Augustine, *Eighty-three Different Questions*, XXXV.2.

34. 1 John 4:18.

35. Harjo, "Emergence," in Harjo, *Map to the Next World*, 29.

36. Ogle, *Politics and the Earthly City*, 134.

constituted by its relationship to others in that order. Thus, each part, in its unique reflection of God's creative grace, serves to enhance the goodness of the whole when it functions according to its proper kind.

When we love excessively or deficiently in light of the cosmological paradigm, our love turns false because we distort the essential being of the other, asserting contrived—and therefore false—reality. When we do not act in ways that fit in with the cosmological whole, we cannot be said to love authentically. "Falsehood," Augustine recognizes, "consists in not living in the way for which [we were] created."[37] Truth, then, is known through love, but love is fulfilled by truth. Augustine defines authentic love as this: "that while holding fast to the truth, we may live justly."[38]

For Augustine, ascent to truth requires "a single course to which the will may apply itself as a single whole, so that it is no longer split into several different wills," especially when "the higher part of our nature aspires after eternal bliss while our lower self is held back by the love of temporal pleasure."[39] Motivating each facet of the self to pursue truth in an integrated way is the function of the virtue of justice: justice works to unify the self, which enables authentic relationship. Augustine recognizes, however, that since human beings tend toward a divided will rather than toward justice, the grace of God recollects us, gathering our scattered selves to more integrated being and drawing us toward oneness.[40]

This dispersion has never been more apparent to me than when I was preparing to defend my dissertation while maintaining responsibility for the full-time care of my toddler and newborn. Though my love for my children is of another sort, writing my dissertation was itself a labor of love; and I found that the amount of attention I wanted to offer to both loves was impossible to dedicate to either.

I realize now that the source of frustration was not that I *had* to split my attention; it was simply that I *wanted* to be fully present to each love, and I could not be. The finitude of our humanity means that we never can love everything in the practical ways we might want to, though our hearts can extend indefinitely. If we can focus instead on the whole toward which our loves are ordered, it can help ease the ache of dispersion—of love that can never express the particular truth of its fullness.

Augustine, too, recognizes the burnout we can experience when the pull of love draws us out of ourselves and we are extended in multiple

---

37. Augustine, *City of God*, XIV.4.
38.. Augustine, *On the Trinity*, VIII.7.10.
39. Augustine, *Confessions*, VII.10.
40. See Augustine, *Confessions*, I.2.

directions. He writes, "It is love of truth that looks for sanctified leisure, while it is the compulsion of love that undertakes righteous engagement in affairs. . . . Yet even in this [latter] case the delight in truth should not be utterly abandoned, for fear that we should lose this enjoyment and that compulsion should overwhelm us."[41] The "righteous engagement" that love of truth motivates indicates efforts to foster right relationships in a world bounded by limits. So, he advises, only when we ground ourselves in the One beyond the many, can we experience the self-integration that allows a fuller expression of our love.[42]

For Augustine, love of God is the source and fulfillment of happiness. When our intellect is able to apprehend the One and remain there in love, we find joy because the multiplicity of our desire is gathered together, and we begin to act with a single purpose that reflects the light of eternity. He writes, "As to virtue leading us to a happy life, I hold virtue to be nothing else than perfect love of God."[43] In other words, as James Wetzel explains, "For Augustine, the return of a soul to God is the heart's return to itself."[44]

When our efforts to express love can be brought into alignment with the One, we are able to express our loves more fully. It is, for Augustine, this vertical/horizontal dynamic that empowers us to broaden the horizons of our love beyond the limits of our own perception—to extend outward as we ascend upward, attending to the authentic reality of the other in relationship.

LOVE'S VULNERABILITY

In Book IV of *Confessions*, Augustine reflects on the character of love through an experience of loss. As he recalls the death of his childhood friend, we see him grapple with what it means to love in a world that thwarts even our most earnest attempts.

Augustine describes his relationship with his friend as one of "sweetness . . . mellowed by the interests [they] shared."[45] However, Augustine departicularizes his friend, describing him, as Richard Miller observes, "not in terms of particularities or peculiarities that mark him off as a distinct individual, but in terms of the two friends' similarities";[46] and, Miller elaborates, "the two young men's similarity is intense; their friendship is less a bonding

41. Augustine, *City of God*, XIX.19.

42. See Niebuhr, *Responsible Self*, 123.

43. Augustine, *On the Morals*, 15.25.

44. Wetzel, "Trappings of Woe," in Wetzel, *Parting Knowledge*, 60.

45. Augustine, *Confessions*, IV.4.

46. Miller, "Evil, Friendship, and Iconic Realism," 393.

of two distinct persons than an absorption of two souls into one, a reduction of identity—both personal and numerical."[47] As Augustine recalls, "I was his second self. . . . I felt that our two souls had become as one, living in two bodies."[48]

Augustine remembers his disconcerting surprise when, prior to Augustine's own conversion, his friend receives the Sacrament of Baptism and rebukes Augustine's attempts to minimize the significance of the event. He struggles to process how it is possible that this friend whom he loves might hold a worldview contrary to his own—how does one continue to love when there is no shared conception of truth?[49]

Upon his friend's death, Augustine describes feeling "utterly lost without him,"[50] writing, "I had become a puzzle to myself."[51] For Augustine, it is because he loved this friend "as though he would never die" that this disorientation occurs.[52] Excessive self-attachment, he realizes, motivated him to possess his friend by projecting his own identity onto his friend, while his failure to attend to his friend's mortality indicates a deficient appreciation of the whole, of which the friend and their relationship were a part. The excess and deficiency of his attachment prevented him from loving the distinct self of his friend.

Without possessing a broader framework for making sense of the world and his relationships, Augustine cannot come to terms with the finitude of his friend. By orienting all experience anthropomorphically and narcissistically toward himself, without reference to a more expansive context, Augustine cannot appreciate the finite otherness of his friend—he misses the realness of his friend's humanity. As Wetzel observes, "Augustine loved his friend in terms that made it impossible for him to have a friend. The consummation of his love would have been, spiritually considered, his friend's death."[53]

47. Miller, "Evil, Friendship, and Iconic Realism," 393. Interestingly, Miller points out that "their relationship mimics in reverse the idea of Christ as two natures in one person" (393).

48. Augustine, *Confessions*, IV.6.

49. This question clearly resonates with contemporary concerns, as there seems to be two distinct versions of reality at work in America today—both sides of the political spectrum maintain the truth of their own, and this is seen in civic discourse (if we can even call it that) as well as internal disagreements in the Church. I believe Augustine's way of making sense of the disconnect can be helpful for us today, and we will return to this question later.

50. Augustine, *Confessions*, IV.4.

51. Augustine, *Confessions*, IV.4.

52. Augustine, *Confessions*, IV.6.

53. Wetzel, "Trappings of Woe," in Wetzel, *Parting Knowledge*, 71.

Because of love's dynamic nature, love draws the lover and beloved toward unity, while perfecting their distinct selves. Love does not cause either over-identification with the other or pure other-regard. The selves of the beloved and the lover should be continuously transformed and made whole by the relational experience of love. Augustine clung to his friend as though his friend would never leave him, but he desired the nearness of his friend so that he himself would be whole, not for his friend's own sake.

Thus, Augustine loved his friend too much, insofar as Augustine depended on him in ways in which he was bound to be disappointed, while simultaneously grounding his love of his friend in his own sense of self, thereby diminishing the particularity of his friend and loving a caricature of him. As Miller puts it, Augustine was in the habit of "homologizing reality to himself, of projecting an anthropomorphic account of power and sovereignty onto the cosmos. As a consequence, he loved his friend as a private possession rather than as someone whose goodness could be shared."[54] This is why Augustine encourages us to love our neighbors with an eye toward the whole: doing so ensures that we have a larger context than ourselves in which to ground our loves. "What madness," Augustine thus exclaims, "to love a man as something more than human!"[55]

Augustine recognizes that his dependency on his friend—his refusal to accept that his friend is distinctively other and distinctively human—distorts his view of reality and, consequently, impedes his ability to love his friend. While "Augustine's onlook toward sensible reality as described in Book 4 was idolatrous,"[56] Miller observes, the mature Augustine possesses an "iconic, theocentric imaginary" that "enables him to perceive mutable goods . . . as disclosively real and truly other."[57]

For me, the tension between iconic and idolatrous love became apparent when we brought our first baby home from the hospital. It had been an unexpected pregnancy, disrupting our first year of doctoral studies, and though there were no major complications, it was not easy on my body. I knew from the first moments spent retching in the bathroom that sacrifice would feature prominently in this new relationship. Still, when we had our initial ultrasound and saw the little one inside me dancing on the screen, I knew I would be willing to make far greater sacrifices in order to reciprocate the joy she embodied. It is amazing to me how love can transform begrudging sacrifice into positive choice.

54. Miller, "Evil, Friendship, and Iconic Realism," 398.
55. Augustine, *Confessions*, IV.7.
56. Miller, "Evil, Friendship, and Iconic Realism," 396.
57. Miller, "Evil, Friendship, and Iconic Realism," 391.

After I labored intensely for nearly forty hours and suffered a life-threatening hemorrhage, in addition to the "usual" physical trauma of childbirth, our daughter made her entrance into this world. When they cut the umbilical cord, my relief was somewhat mixed with grief: the visceral interconnection my daughter and I shared was severed, and our relationship was now entirely different. Mothering her well, I realized then, means raising her to be her own person: it means losing her in small ways, daily. It also means being open to sharing her love with others.

In his grief, Augustine is consoled by the passage of time: "Time never stands still," he writes, "nor does it idly pass by without effect upon our feelings or fail to work its wonders on the mind. It came and went, day after day, and as it passed it filled me with fresh hope and new thoughts to remember. Little by little it pieced me together again."[58] Applied to circumstances of acute loss, these lines offer profound insight. But it is not clear to me that time is an ally to a mother's love. Indeed, Augustine tells of his own mother's struggle to accept his independence, describing her as "wild with grief," because "she loved to have [him] with her, and she did not know what joys you had in store for her because of [his] departure."[59]

Time itself brings continuous loss although, in a paradox Augustine captures so well, it also ushers in new ways of being: "the beauty of the ages," he tells us, "is unfolded in the coming and passing of things."[60] Considering the passage of time through the lens of motherhood thus emphasizes the tension between love's constancy and love's vulnerability: I miss the undiminished innocence of my little ones and our intermingled coexistence, even as I admire their tenacious pursuit of independence. Robin Wall Kimmerer describes this poignantly: "It is the fundamental unfairness of parenting that if we do our jobs well, the deepest bond we are given will walk out the door with a wave over the shoulder."[61]

Perhaps, though, there is consolation despite, or even because of, this tension. The passage of time forces me to love in a way that relinquishes control. It is impossible to do otherwise—"time never stands still." As a prerequisite for receiving the gift of love that is the bond I share with my children, I must be vulnerable to the pain of distinction—to suffering their outward orientation and overcoming my tendency to project myself onto them or to subsume them into my own identity. Still, the love we share

---

58. Augustine, *Confessions*, IV.8.

59. Augustine, *Confessions*, V.8.

60. Augustine, "On the Literal Interpretation," 1.8.14, in Augustine, *On Genesis*.

61. Kimmerer, *Braiding Sweetgrass*, 98.

traverses time and space, so that whatever changes their growth (or mine) motivates, love remains constant.

Encountering my children within a transcendent horizon, rather than confining our relationship to the limited parameters of my personal desires, allows me to recognize these losses as gains—to live in love, not fear. As they grow apart from me, they grow into themselves, and they form more expansive relationships. Indeed, when I was pregnant with my second and third children, I found it difficult to imagine how the love I felt for my eldest could be replicated. But I soon discovered that love cannot be divvied up; it can only overflow.

When we try to limit our love, or cling possessively to the subject of our love so that we refuse to open our hearts to others, the love turns false. Love can only result in more love—in sharing gifts and generating new bonds. If I can open my heart to the pain of losing my children as my "second self"—if I can let go of my idea of them—there will be joy in knowing them as "disclosively real and truly other."

These questions of what it means to love and suffer loss have taken on new contours during our training to become foster parents. By welcoming a child into our family, and sharing our love wholeheartedly, we open ourselves to the imminent loss that will occur when the child is reunited with his biological family or adopted into a forever home. And yet, the gift of a particular child, and the ways she will enliven our family, will make us whole in a way we did not know we needed—and which, if left unfilled, we likely would not notice. But once that bond is forged, we will remain connected. Heartrending loss is a reflection of love shared, which leaves an indelible mark.

My self bears the imprint of my family—physically, emotionally, and spiritually. I am constituted in part by my relationship to them as wife and mother, but also by my relationship to them as individual human beings who have deeply affected my worldview. And my children, I am sure, will never be free from the nature and nurture of myself and my husband. Our ways of being in the world will forever be influenced by one another, and without each other, we would not be fully ourselves. And to the extent that we offer ourselves in love to the many people and projects beyond our immediate family unit, we are changed by and help to transform those, as well. As Kimmerer puts it, "being a good mother doesn't end with creating a home where just my children can flourish. A good mother grows into a richly eutrophic old woman, knowing that her work doesn't end until she creates a home where all of life's beings can flourish."[62] Love, the eternal one, unites us all.

62. Kimmerer, *Braiding Sweetgrass*, 97.

LOVE'S LIMITS

But can we reconcile the conviction that expansive encounter is the key to wholeness with the recognition that personal boundaries are important, too? I think so. It is perhaps similar to determining when my child is old enough to go down the big slide, or cross the street alone. It involves a tenuous balance between maintaining boundaries for safety, while recognizing that holding on too tightly will thwart a child's development.

All creatures, in our uniqueness, have gifts to offer the world. As Edward Collins Vacek claims, "the contribution that each of us makes to justice or peace is irreplaceable. It is not an empty tautology to assert that without me God cannot do what God does through me."[63] While we should remain open to expansive encounter and the particular gifts embodied by our neighbors, it is prudent to recognize that sometimes the dignity we bring to such encounters is threatened because we are situated in a world perverted by the lust for domination. Among such disordered relationships, discerning what is necessary for protection is appropriate, though prudence, not fear, should characterize our actions.

Our attitude toward our neighbors should be one that hopes that they too will share in—and be integral to—peace. And this entails an openness to personal growth and to the expansion of our own imaginative horizons. I should emphasize, here, that because love is the condition for the possibility of justice that fosters flourishing beyond simply recognizing rights, the internal motivations and emotions with which we act are morally relevant. Love never demands that we subjugate our dignity to preserve the pride of another; but at the same time, love will not generate hostility. Actions performed without love—or that lack the affective posture that lend them sincerity—cannot foster right relationships.

So, when my son hits his sister, I move her away from the situation so she does not get hurt, and I remind him that if he does not respect the integrity of her body, then he will not be permitted to play with her. The natural consequence reinforces to him that the respect that comes from love serves a happier end than his self-serving mode of control. When he apologizes and they embrace, they learn that love requires limits, and that love remains ever hopeful.

And here we see an infantile episode of the distinction between the torment of hell and the peace of heaven: feeling one's love to be truncated by imposed barriers versus flourishing in the freedom that love makes possible. When the yearning of the human heart is misdirected, it mistakes limits for

63. Vacek, *Love, Human and Divine*, 104.

SEEKING TRUTH WITH SAINT AUGUSTINE   31

rejection and views boundaries as stifling. It is frustrating for our love to be curtailed, but when we love authentically, limits appear not as limits at all but as the means of flourishing according to the order prescribed by truth. Sacrifice can become positive choice when we expand the horizons of our love.

Augustine holds that sin manifests in our inability to maintain this balance of love. Because of sin, he argues, our intellect becomes distracted from attaining the heights of truth—oneness—and we begin to pursue lower, finite and temporal, goods. Without God, the transience of life becomes overwhelming; we are scattered and distended as we seek an object that can sustain the eternal love of our hearts. But when we "rest in God," all things are brought into proper perspective, flourishing in interrelationship. In Augustine's thought, as Wetzel has noted, "the heart is a transgressive organ. . . . The odd business of living outside one's body—familiar to anyone with a heart—finally makes sense in relation to God, the inexhaustible being whose otherness is the heart's food."[64]

By ordering our love according to truth, we broaden the horizons of our love beyond the limits of our own perception and are thereby able to accommodate the authentic freedom of the other. For human beings, whose love is always somewhat awry, love that requires us to relinquish control is torturous, but remaining open to it is to participate in the love of Christ and the life of the Spirit—the "love that is shed abroad in our hearts."[65]

This is why Augustine identifies sin with a rejection of relational goods in favor of pride, or an individualistic sense of autonomy, noting that sin manifests in becoming a person *incurvatus in se*: turned in on oneself.[66] This curving inward distorts our ability to love, which in turn distorts our ability to seek truth: "The self erects buffers and barriers to preserve its freedom," Paul Camacho observes, "but after all of its building it looks up to find that it is enclosed within a small cell of its own making. Is this the deepest meaning of freedom: not liberty, but self-imprisonment?"[67] We are made to delight in truth, but we are inhibited from apprehending its fullness; our efforts are limited by our humanity, though we are compelled by love's eternal striving. Losing sight of this dynamic can stunt our own moral development and lead us to self-righteous—or fearful—obstinacy rather than open encounter.

64. Wetzel, "Crisis Mentalities," in Wetzel, *Parting Knowledge*, 28.
65. Rom 5:5.
66. Augustine, *City of God*, XII.6.
67. Camacho, "Weight of Love," 2.

CONVERSION COMPLETE?

So it was that I learned to associate faith with intellectual delight, and to cope with love's vulnerability through ordering my desires according to the hierarchy of goods, in pursuit of absolute truth. As I explored Augustine's thought and the Catholic tradition, I gradually submitted more and more fully to the Magisterium—I tried hard to internalize the catechism and to defend the church's moral teaching against the danger of relativism. If the church is the repository of truth, I reasoned, then to order my loves according to truth requires this submission. I used to joke that every year I became more Catholic as I discovered and tried to implement an increasing number of personal faith practices. (My favorite thus far is the Advent wreath, though—at the risk of appalling some readers—I confess that I have not yet attempted Adoration.)

Embracing a tradition that has stood for millennia and encompasses people around the globe offers a vantage point that necessitates wide moral vision. Despite its limits and failures, the church, with its sacraments and rituals, serves as a reminder that I am not the source or even the center of my life; I am but one integral part of a community that journeys toward the whole, embodied in Christ.

Fresh from the achievement of earning my doctoral degree, I also began teaching theology and ethics courses to undergraduate students who were for the most part required to take the classes to satisfy core requirements. At the time, I was excited about the opportunity to share my mastery of the subjects and the insights I had discovered through writing my dissertation: that truth should constrain love, and that Augustine's model of right relationships—envisaged according to a hierarchical order—offers a sound framework for contemporary ethics. In other words, I taught in a way that imposed knowledge, rather than one that invited exploration (my *libido dominandi* at work, it seems). My efforts left me unfulfilled, and I imagine my students were not overly excited to come to class.

After a few years of this uninspired teaching experience, I left the known order of the academic world to join the staff of an order of women religious. There, I met some of the most inspiring women I have ever encountered as they toiled in the trenches of ministry. The dedication of women religious to Christ, exemplified through solidarity with the vulnerable, prompted me to question whether becoming "more Catholic" has more to do with submitting to the institution of the church, or to fostering right relationships through expansive encounter. Theoretically, the two never should be in tension; and yet, the division that marks the witness of the church today suggests a disconnect.

PAUSE FOR REFLECTION

Take a moment to reflect on what you read.

- What is drawing your attention? What words, phrases, or concepts stand out to you? Are any new insights stirring in you?

- When have you experienced an encounter that challenged an ideal you held?

- When have you experienced a conversion? Who or what helped to inspire it? How did your new way of being resonate with your previously held values?

- *Augustine recognizes that it is love that moves us toward truth and inspires us to remain in its light. It is also love that leads us astray and makes us willing to be deceived.* As you reflect on these words, what experience in your life comes to mind?

2

Recovering Tradition with Women of the Church

A Spiritual Conversion

The blood was watery, flowing from Mama, flowing from my eyes.

Later, at dinner, Papa said we would recite sixteen different novenas.
For Mama's forgiveness. . . . I did not think, I did not even think to
think, what Mama needed to be forgiven for.

—CHIMAMANDA NGOZI ADICHIE, *PURPLE HIBISCUS*

I HAPPENED SERENDIPITOUSLY UPON the job advertisement for the assistant director of the Office of Justice, Peace, and Integrity of Creation in
the Atlantic-Midwest Province of the School Sisters of Notre Dame, and I
applied with the hope of putting my education to use outside of the classroom. During my interview, I discovered that the SSND trace their spiritual
heritage to Saint Augustine, "who formed a community to be of one mind
and one heart, and who took the Trinity to be the basis, source, and goal of
community."[1] The charism of the SSND—their transformative grace to share

1. School Sisters of Notre Dame, "Constitution," Prologue, in *You Are Sent*. Note
that other sources of the SSND spiritual heritage include Alix Le Clerc, Peter Fourier,

with the church and the world—is unity, and they "direct their entire lives toward that oneness for which Jesus Christ was sent."[2] Their way of engaging in right relationships ordered toward oneness offers a rich interpretation of Augustinian spirituality that transformed my way of being Catholic and expanded my worldview by reimagining faith in terms of interconnection, rather than hierarchy.

When I first applied for the job, the language of oneness made me wary. Was "oneness" merely code for the relativistic, radical inclusion that watered down authentic Catholicism? I wondered. But I took the job with conviction that we could find common ground in the cause for justice since our Catholic faith and Augustine's spirituality grounded us. Later, I would realize that radical inclusion is not insipid, nor must it be relativistic—the call to oneness issues from Christ.

I became open to entertaining this realization during a fellowship I received the semester prior, just after my youngest daughter was born. I worked with the Education for Justice Project (EFJ), a project of the Center of Concern in Washington, DC,[3] where I developed a series of articles that explored human rights through the lens of Catholic social thought. Each piece of the series focused on a particular issue of contemporary concern in light of the teachings of our church.

In the planning—which occurred largely between midnight and 6 a.m., when I was awake to nurse the little one but her older siblings, still toddlers, were sleeping—I focused my attention on hot-button cultural issues like abortion, homosexuality, and gender identity. Compelled by the zeal of a convert with newly developed academic expertise, I decided to write the series on keeping rightly ordered love and right relationships at the forefront of concern: we Catholics need to maintain a posture of compassion and respect, but also a firm line against sin. As Augustine pointedly asks Nectarius in a letter, "would you prefer your home-town to flower with piety or with license, with reformed characters or with atrocities unchecked? Compare the choices and see whether . . . you, or we, are more fully and genuinely eager for it to flourish."[4]

At the time, I was unaware of how often this sentiment has been used as a cudgel to justify harms inflicted when piety is defined according to a hierarchical worldview. I was surprised, then, when my topics were rejected

---

Michael Wittman, Francis Sebastian Job, and Mother Caroline Friess, SSND.

2. School Sisters of Notre Dame, "Constitution," in *You Are Sent*, 4.

3. The Education for Justice Project is now under the umbrella of the Ignatian Solidarity Network.

4. Augustine, *Ep.* 91.2, in *Augustine: Political Writings*.

and the staff at EFJ suggested that I write instead about issues such as climate change, immigration, and violence against women. What, I wondered, did education for justice mean if we were not advocating for the issues designated by the clerical hierarchy as preeminent concerns to the church? What would distinguish our work from that of our secular counterparts?

Nevertheless, I agreed, still determined to infuse the internal order our faith inspires into the external application. When I wrote on violence against women, for example, I reminded readers of the "feminine genius"— an affirmation of the essential nature of women taught by St. Pope John Paul II. But upon receiving the draft, my director, Dianna Ortiz, OSU, asked me gently but pointedly whether I had ever explored theological affirmations of women that were developed *by women*.

I am rather embarrassed to admit that during all my years of graduate studies, I had not, in fact, considered whether women might have anything particular to say about dignity and personhood that could enrich the teachings of the church. Not that I thought women should be actively excluded, and of course I recognized myself as a woman participating in such theological discourse; it just never occurred to me that it might matter whose voices were contributing to the development of our faith tradition. As I researched and reflected, I began to feel an internal shift—a conversion—akin to what I experienced when I visited Graterford Penitentiary: a sense that my worldview was limited, and I had much to learn.

Later, I found out that Sister Dianna had spent much of her life as a leading advocate against torture. After experiencing her own trauma of kidnapping, rape, and torture at the hands of a Guatemalan security force, she committed herself to opposing torture methods implemented by the United States government, including engaging in a five-week hunger strike that resulted in the release of documents related to the government's involvement in equipping and training right-wing Guatemalan military forces that were guilty of genocide and other human rights abuses.[5]

Sister Dianna died in 2021, and I count it among life's greatest blessings that I knew her. I have a photo of her planting a kiss on the top of my daughter's head, and it is this sweet image that captures, for me, the gentle strength and fierce grace that Sister Dianna embodied. If only I had been more intentional about learning from *her* what it means to affirm the dignity of women.

Because of her influence, when I joined the staff of the SSND, I was open—slightly—to experiencing a transformation of consciousness. As I

5. To learn her story in her own words, see Sister Dianna's autobiography, *The Blindfold's Eyes*.

began to form relationships with the SSND community, I sensed that I was working out of a worldview that differed from theirs, though I struggled to put my finger on why, since we were moved by our shared Catholic faith to work together for peace and justice.

My view of rightly ordered love recognized, of course, that interior virtue would manifest in action for justice; and the Augustinian theology of right relationships certainly motivated me to advocate on behalf of the marginalized, and to prioritize, for example, the spiritual relationship of neighbor over the human constructs of race and nationality. Still, I noticed dissimilarities between the Catholicism I had been living and the Catholicity of the Sisters, and I know now that it came down to this: my Catholicism was ordered toward absolute truth; theirs was a Catholicity ordered toward encounter. I observed the sisters, time and again, reach out to encounter those who were oppressed and reflect on the meaning of that encounter for their interior lives. They saw Christ in others first; I sought to bring Christ to others. A subtle difference, but a crucial one that illuminated a new way to assess what is "distinctively Christian" about the work for justice.

Once, after I had given a presentation on an Augustinian spirituality of rightly ordered love and right relationships, one of the sisters pulled me aside for a chat. She was intrigued by what I had said and wanted to probe Augustine's thought a bit more deeply. It was a lovely conversation, but I suspect I was affected more than she. I left with her words resounding in my head: "I think God probably laughs at our efforts at piety," she confided. "God is so much bigger than this."

This startling spiritual insight offered so unassumingly from a Catholic nun began to sink into my heart as I watched the sisters order their lives toward unity, grounded in trinitarian spirituality and embodied through special concern for those who are poor or marginalized. Indeed, I received that special concern as a new mother.

While my motherly identity might have been overlooked or denigrated in other places of employ, the SSND community affirmed me in it. They did not make me choose between excelling in a career and being the kind of mother I wished to be. From offering a private room where I could pump breast milk for my infant daughter, to allowing me to adjust my work hours according to my family's needs, to permitting me to work remotely when needed (before working remotely was a widespread necessity), to showing general interest and enthusiasm in matters regarding my kids: I was made to feel welcome. Their flexibility and support made space for me to share my gifts in the public realm, while prioritizing my life as a mother at home. There, I experienced an authentic affirmation of the dignity of women.

Early on in my tenure with the SSND, I wrote an essay entitled "Partnership as a Model for Mission: Lessons on Solidarity from Augustine and the School Sisters of Notre Dame."[6] In it, I tried to tease out the features of Augustine's account that helped to undergird the ministry of the SSND, particularly in their partnership with Beyond Borders, an NGO working for sustainable development with Haitian communities. Rightly ordered love helps us recognize the equal dignity of all human beings, I argued. We are interconnected in a hierarchy of being, and this should motivate us to act in solidarity for the flourishing of all—indeed, our own flourishing is bound up with that of our neighbors.

The article was well-received by the SSND community, but some of the feedback questioned the use of a model of hierarchy for promoting dignity. I fielded pointed critiques that emphasized the dangers of a hierarchical worldview, noting that hierarchical structures had been invoked by Catholics to justify slavery, genocide, misogyny, and ecological trauma throughout history. Others observed indignantly that I had neglected to transpose Augustine's use of masculine terms for God into gender-neutral phrasing. How could we overcome dominative habits, they asked, if the language we use reinforces patriarchal domination? The vehemence of these critiques gave me pause and moved me to consider whether there might be something to them.

I found that although Augustine's theology of love requires right relationships for its full expression—love is impoverished without justice, and justice is incomplete without love—it nevertheless undermines this crucial human insight by assuming a hierarchy that maintains the dominance of human beings (men, in particular). Augustine himself recognizes that sin inheres in the pursuit of power, so ordering our loves according to a dominative structure inevitably will complicate the pursuit of right relationships. As I learned how a paradigm of patriarchal hierarchy has been and remains harmful, I began to develop a richer understanding of what it might mean for relationships to be *right*.

HIERARCHY, PATRIARCHY, AND WOMEN IN THE CHURCH

Augustine's view of order and ascent to the One is shaped by his understanding of the cosmos—of the relation of parts in light of the whole. However, Peter Brown laments that Augustine "allowed the Platonic sense of the

6. Bonnette, "Partnership as a Model."

majesty of the *cosmos* to grow pale. Lost in the narrow and ever fascinating labyrinth of his preoccupation with the human will," Brown observes,

> Augustine turned his back on the *mundus*, on the magical beauty associated with the material universe in later Platonism. . . . He was, of course, convinced that the order of the *mundus* reminded human beings of the wisdom and power of their Creator. But Augustine would never look up at the stars and gaze at the world around him with the shudder of religious awe that fell upon Plotinus, when he exclaimed . . . "All the place is holy" (as Oedipus had exclaimed at Colonus, and as Jacob had done at Bethel: *Surely the Lord is in this place* [Gen. 28:16]). Plotinus went on to write of the *cosmos*: "and there is nothing in it which is without a share of soul." Augustine pointedly refused to share this enthusiasm. . . . Something was lost, in Western Christendom, by this trenchant and seemingly commonsensical judgment.[7]

Indeed, Andrea Nightingale argues that "Augustine is rich in refusals—refusals to see and know the earthly world. He vigorously turns away from the bodily realm, which offers nothing but sinful distraction."[8] I am more inclined to read notes of wonder in Augustine's texts—he waxes eloquently on the beauty of creation more than once. Unfortunately for him, the hierarchy that constrains his imagination inhibits his ability to appreciate, fully, the goodness of earthly life—he is focused on "higher" things.

Ilia Delio observes the implications of this for the church: "In the first five centuries of the Church," in part due to Augustine's influence, there was "a mutation of catholicity from a sense of the cosmos as order and harmony to a fixation on orthodoxy."[9] Augustine's limited cosmological awareness helped to justify "the Church [becoming] defined as *Catholic* not with a sense of the whole but with a sense of the true."[10] The whole opens our imaginative horizons; the true suggests that there is a fixed goal of apprehension. Certainly, truth is a feature of goodness and beauty—the true grounds us in what is real and enables communication, which is essential for relationships. But when we take our convictions to be the ultimate goal of our love, we distort love's true essence: unity-in-difference.

Although Augustine recognizes that all human beings are equal in the cosmological order by nature, he proposes a social order that reinforces the dominance of human beings over the rest of creation and affirms the inequity

---

7. Brown, *Augustine of Hippo*, 504.
8. Nightingale, *Once Out of Nature*, 7. See Augustine, *Confessions*, X.35.
9. Delio, *Making All Things New*, 16.
10. Delio, *Making All Things New*, 14.

of a patriarchal—or male-dominated—system, against which persons who are non-male, non-white, and non-Western have had to struggle for millenia. Though we certainly cannot place the blame for oppressive patriarchal structures squarely on his shoulders—they existed long before his time and likely would have continued without his influence—it is important to grapple with the ways in which Augustine's theology lends itself to the perpetuation of such structures, before considering how it can help rectify them.[11]

Augustine's thought has been remarkably influential on church-state relations and Christian doctrine, generally, and though we might attribute its success to his brilliance or genuine humanistic intuitions, we must reckon with the misogyny that is woven throughout his work since it informs contemporary worldviews. Carol Gilligan, for example, credits the "remarkable success" of Augustine's thought to the usefulness of his theology for sustaining "a patriarchal conception of authority" after the collapse of the Roman empire.[12] Of course, as Ann Matter reminds us, "Augustine's ideas about women developed in a particular context in which he was struggling with particular theological constructs. . . . No theological framework can be divorced from the particularities of the world that shaped it."[13] Importantly, she suggests, "This is a lesson that institutional Christianity is still struggling to learn."[14]

While Augustine's emphases on right relationships and humility might temper any tendency toward domination that could be garnered from his thought, his cosmological framework is built on a hierarchy of goods, which lends itself to projections of superiority and a limited understanding of humility. Further, he does not challenge the patriarchal structures of his day in a significant way. Indeed, Judith Chelius Stark laments that "although Augustine had the conceptual tools and lines of argument available to affirm the image of God in women in a much less conditional way than he did, he did not do so. Why does he fail to affirm women's imago status," she asks, "when his own project . . . gave him a powerful paradigm with which to overcome the hierarchical thinking and rigid dualities that led to his narrow and highly qualified view of women?"[15]

In other words, in Augustine's thought we find tools to build an ethic of equality and interconnection, but his general acquiescence to Roman

11. For a thorough historical account of the origins and perpetuation of patriarchy, see Lerner, *Creation of Patriarchy*.

12. Gilligan, *Deepening Darkness*, 112.

13. Matter, "*De cura feminarum*," in Stark, *Feminist Interpretations*, 210.

14. Matter, "*De cura feminarum*," in Stark, *Feminist Interpretations*, 210.

15. Stark, "Augustine on Women," in Stark, *Feminist Interpretations*, 217.

patriarchy, combined with the cosmological framework of hierarchy he maintains, deter him from building such an ethic himself; and we should not be surprised that many interpreters of his thought have ignored or mis-read the demands of humility and friendship since they often work within the constraints of this paradigm of hierarchy. Recovering and enriching these demands will be a primary focus in subsequent chapters, but in what follows, I want to examine some of the dominative tendencies of Augustine's theology and the way in which they have been interpreted and passed down.

In much of his work, Augustine maintains that women are socially in-ferior to men. Augustine tells us that in their physical, sexed, and gendered bodies, women do not bear the image of God—it is only imprinted on the rational parts of their souls, which are ordered toward eternal truth. Men, of course, reflect *imago dei* unconditionally, inclusive of their embodied sex and gender. Interpreting Saint Paul, for example, Augustine argues that "as regards the different sex of two human beings, he assigns the image of God only to the man and not to the woman."[16] This sentiment underlies the ori-gin of women wearing head coverings in Mass: their bodies do not image God and must be hidden. It is also one reason women have been excluded from the clerical priesthood.[17] And I learned from the sisters that contem-porary notions of male/female complementarity likely originate from this assumption that women do not image God fully, apart from their relation-ship to men.

Stark explains that "Augustine has admitted that women as human beings (*homo*) are made in God's image—in the ontological and spiritual senses, but not as women per se (*femina*). This emphasis on the spiritual imago status is consistent with Augustine's hierarchical way of thinking about reality."[18] Though Augustine recognizes that women participate in the image of God insofar as they are human, he also maintains that their imaging of God must be constrained and ordered by their relationship to (superior) males, just as our bodily desires must be ordered and constrained by rational truth.

Indeed, Augustine extrapolates from his cosmological sensibility to claim that an ordered domestic life should reflect a hierarchy wherein women, children, and slaves submit to the male head of household.[19] But this, of course, is for their own good, since to live a life of disorder prevents one from flourishing. As Oliver O'Donovan explains, "So seriously, in fact,

16. Augustine, *On the Trinity*, 12.19.
17. See Congregation for the Doctrine of the Faith, "*Inter Insigniores*."
18. Stark, "Augustine on Women," in Stark, *Feminist Interpretations*, 234.
19. Augustine, *City of God*, XIX.14.

does Augustine take the ontological hierarchy of goods—the good of the soul is God, the good of the body the soul—that it is quite impossible to discern any substantial difference between love of the soul and love of the body. . . . True love of the flesh commits us to that subordination of matter to spirit which will enable the soul to resist the faults of the flesh. Then it is that the flesh is properly cared for."[20]

This sentiment has shown up consistently throughout church history in efforts to save souls. We see it in the church's sanctioning of Native American genocide through the so-called Doctrine of Discovery,[21] and in its subsequent participation in boarding schools and other efforts to "kill the Indian, but save the man";[22] we see it in the church's participation in the transatlantic slave trade.[23] Indeed, Tiya Miles's description of the prevailing consciousness of the slaveholding United States is illuminating:

> The upper classes had long adopted a frame of mind, often referred to as "paternalism," that allowed them to feel that slaveholding was morally right and even benevolent. . . . Elites believed in the correctness of a hierarchical social structure that they understood as being not only natural but also ordained by God. To them, the world was strictly ordered, with a proper place for everyone in it: a select few at the top would dominate and take responsibility for a vast mass of dependents below. In this eighteenth-century paternalistic vision of a stable, organized society bolstered by an early-nineteenth century Christian revivalism, landholding white men maintained the right to control those beneath them in status, even and especially loved ones within the household.[24]

Like Augustine's conception of social order, this worldview, too, was rooted in the same theological paradigm that affirmed a hierarchical cosmos: "Just as God reigned over his creation with the carrot of heaven and the stick of hell," Miles writes, "the white male father figure governed the dependent inhabitants of his household. . . . The ethos of paternalism legitimized slavery by suggesting that the slave order was organic and right."[25]

---

20. O'Donovan, *Problem of Self-Love*, 47.

21. See Alexander VI, *Inter Caetera*.

22. See Pratt, "Advantages of Mingling," in Barrows, *Proceedings of the National Conference*, 46; and the Editors of *America: The Jesuit Review*, "Catholic Church Must Come Clean."

23. Williams, "Black Catholic Women."

24. Miles, *All That She Carried*, 84.

25. Miles, *All That She Carried*, 84.

Importantly, Rosemary Radford Ruether recognizes, paradigms of hierarchy result in "the ruling class [inscribing] in the systems of law, philosophy, and theology a 'master narrative' or 'logic of domination' that defines the normative human in terms of this male ruling group."[26] And Ada María Isasi-Díaz concurs: "The dominant group, the group that has power, considers oppressed people as having no value or significance. Those who are oppressed . . . are not taken into consideration in determining what is normative for society."[27]

When our worldview is based on hierarchy, we balk at attempts to challenge those at the top, who dictate what we consider normative—but it should be clear that, sometimes, those in power get it wrong, with devastating consequences for the "inferior" masses. This is what Sister Thea Bowman called to the church's attention in 1989, when she lamented that if Black Catholics "attempt to bring our blackism to the church, the people who do not know us say that we are being 'non-Catholic' or 'Separatist'—or just plain 'uncouth.'"[28] In other words, it matters who is interpreting our faith or defining "order."

And certainly, it is not only human persons who have been subjected to violence sanctioned by a distorted sense of order that was assumed to be divinely ordained. Noting the connection between patriarchy and environmental injustice, Ladonna Brave Bull Allard explains that "the abuse against women is well known in American history, world history—and this tells you a lot about what is happening to our Earth."[29] Elizabeth A. Johnson, CSJ, describes the implications: "In the dualistic framework, the physically fecund powers of both women and the earth are ontologically inferior to the rational mind. They are meant to serve men's needs for progeny and life maintaining skills. At the same time men must struggle against the flesh, change and death which these elements represent. The resulting worldview subordinates both women and earth to men's control, which can turn violent and exploitative with little compunction."[30] The natural world has been harmed irreparably, thanks to the human tendency toward mastery, which has been mediated through religious traditions that emphasize hierarchy and sanction dominance.

26. Ruether, "Ecofeminist Philosophy," in Kearns and Keller, *Ecospirit*, 78.

27. Isasi-Díaz, "Mujerista Discourse," in Isasi-Díaz and Mendieta, *Decolonizing Epistemologies*, 46.

28. Bowman, "Address to the U.S. Bishop's Conference."

29. Citron-Fink, "One Mom's Story."

30. Johnson, *Ask the Beasts*, 126.

Catherine Keller and Laurel Kearns, critiquing "ideology that exploits and discards the nonhumans along with the majority of the humans, and the spiritual ideologies that legitimate it by collusion or default," recognize that "predominant among these spiritual ideologies is a Christendom that has tended to trade its own body-affirmative potentials—encoded in the doctrines of creation, incarnation, and resurrection—for body-denigrating priorities. It has intensified human 'dominion' over the other creatures by way of a naturalized dualism of spirit over flesh, of a supernatural heaven over a material earth."[31]

While Augustine insists that our material bodies are goods to be valued, he blames disordered physical desires for sin and dissatisfaction—and he implies that those corporeal desires are made to appear desirable through the seductive powers of women. He writes, for example, that the serpent "had a deceitful conversation with the woman—no doubt starting with the inferior of the human pair so as to arrive at the whole by stages, supposing the man would not be so easily gullible, and could not be trapped by a false move on his own part, but only if he yielded to another's mistake."[32]

It is hard to gloss over such explicit misogyny. Augustine does maintain that those with more authority ought to use it in service of their subjects, and certainly, if interpreters of Augustine had attended more robustly to his insistence on this, perhaps the oppressive nature of hierarchies in the church and society could have been mitigated. However, though he acknowledges that human nature confers dignity, it remains the case that Augustine ascribes superiority to some people through the justification of divine order—this gives those in power the divine right to determine who counts as human, who counts as important, and who counts as worthy of respect. We have seen the dangers of assigning to a select few the right to define who or what counts as valuable.

Again—if there is a hierarchy, we humans want to be at the top. Augustine articulates this insightfully. Unfortunately, it seems he neglected to incorporate this insight into his view of social relations. Augustine's conception of the good life as one in which men—with the rare exception of idealized, asexualized women like his mother Monica—engage in "scintillating conversation" to ascend to God, while attempting to avoid the entrapment of women's sexuality, helped to produce what Gilligan calls the "ultimate

---

31. Keller and Kearns, "Introduction: Grounding Theory," in Kearns and Keller, *Ecospirit*, 4.

32. Augustine, *City of God*, XIV.11.

form of religio-ethical patriarchy: a rule of male, celibate priests to whom all others are subordinate."[33]

Whether or not Augustine intended this outcome is somewhat beside the point: it is a fairly straightforward endeavor to construct such justification from his thought and the misogynistic sentiments it contains. Augustine shares his views quite plainly: "If God had wanted Adam to have a partner in scintillating conversation he would have created another man; the fact that God created a woman showed that he had in mind the survival of the human race."[34] And though we might try to ignore or excise such language from Augustine's legacy, we must reckon with the fact that this sentiment has seeped insidiously into the structures of our church.

Carole Ganim—a former religious sister—identifies the influence of this patriarchal hierarchy in the contemporary experience of her vow of chastity, which she eventually came to reject:

> We vowed chastity to free ourselves from deep human attachments so we might be dedicated to God. We left our homes and our family in order to live a more perfect life, to enter into the "State of Perfection" and to serve people in the name of Jesus. Certainly, this kind of dedication was praiseworthy, and in many ways it did allow more freedom to serve others. The downfall, however, of such a vow was that it effectively denied our humanity. Chastity denied not only sexuality but also all the relationships that demand a personal, affectional commitment of one person to another. This often resulted in distance from emotion and attachment to self. Some of us were self-absorbed, cold, uncaring. Others were just dried up like Langston Hughes's "raisin in the sun." As chastity became spiritualized as a vow rejecting one's sinful flesh in order to be purified, the vow also became an instrument of control of women within the Church.[35]

---

33. Gilligan, *Deepening Darkness*, 113.

34. Augustine, *Literal Commentary on Genesis,* cited in Chadwick, *Saint Augustine's Confessions,* xviii. Note that elsewhere Augustine does recognize marriage as "friendship," in the sense of loving "the good of friends as much as its own, and for their sake wishes for them what it wishes for itself," (Augustine, *City of God,* XIX.3, cited in Clair, "Interlude: Augustinian *Oikeiōsis*," in *Discerning the Good,* 43). Though these kinds of seemingly contradictory statements might make it difficult to identify Augustine's "actual view" of women, I submit that even the fluctuation between such statements demonstrates misogyny at work—that he feels justified in either affirming or denigrating the place of women in friendship seems to come out of a problematic posture toward women.

35. Ganim, "Unruly Women," in DelRosso, *Unruly Catholic Nuns,* 57.

Importantly, not all religious orders adopted vows of chastity to reject the sinful flesh. As Shannen Dee Williams details in her groundbreaking study of Black women religious, at the newly founded National Black Sisters Conference (NBSC) in 1970, delegates "renewed their vows of celibacy, noting their utility in such times of great social change and upheaval."[36] Williams recounts the address of Sister of the Holy Family Theresa Perry, who "linked celibacy to Black freedom, saying, 'To be celibate means that we have dedicated ourselves totally and completely to building the new . . . to ushering in the future. . . . The challenge is to free yourself enough so you can free other people.'"[37]

These women religious, it seems, adopted celibacy not for the sake of their souls or in deference to masculine conceptions of purity, but to reclaim the agency of their bodies and other bodies marginalized by religious, social, and political injustice. Williams observes: "In declaring celibacy an act of Black liberation, NBSC members powerfully challenged the masculinist ethos of certain segments of the Black protest community that regarded Black women as able to contribute only through motherhood. In demonstrating themselves to be formidable leaders in the Catholic fight for racial justice, they also challenged the misogyny and sexism of many of their male counterparts who had initially believed Black sisters needed to stand behind Black priests in their quest for Black power in the Church."[38]

We see a related witness embodied by Chicana and Latina sisters, who, Lara Medina notes, "transformed religious life to be intimately connected to the struggles of their ethnic and gendered communities."[39] Indeed, in her study of Las Hermanas, a national organization for Hispanic Catholic women, Medina recognizes that "their distinct arena, the sanctified patriarchy of the Catholic Church, made them keenly aware of the forces of male domination. The women of Las Hermanas defy long-standing stereotypes of Latina Catholics as apolitical and asexual passive bearers of their faith."[40] By asserting the dignity of their bodies and connecting embodied struggle directly to faith practice, these women of color offered a counter paradigm to the hierarchical framework that denigrated their bodies and subjugated them to those who were male and/or white.

Augustine's ideal of bodies subjugated to souls, and women subjugated to men, seems to have perpetuated, or at least sustained, this paradigm, this

---

36. Williams, *Subversive Habits*, 198.
37. Williams, *Subversive Habits*, 198.
38. Williams, *Subversive Habits*, 198.
39. Medina, *Las Hermanas*, 1.
40. Medina, *Las Hermanas*, 2.

conception of order that offers justification for "religious intolerance that represses any voice that does not conform to patriarchal authority."[41] St. Teresa of Ávila, Doctor of the Church, described the matter bluntly in the sixteenth century: "Since the world's judges are sons of Adam and all of them men, there is no virtue in women that they do not hold suspect."[42] And Williams recognizes that this sentiment has been compounded for Black women in the United States: "the vehemence with which white Catholics opposed the very idea of Black sisters and characterized them as morally suspect is abundantly documented. . . . In a white-dominated and patriarchal society and Church that often opposed interracial marriage in law and custom, the very idea of a Black bride of a Christ imagined as white was nothing short of insurrectionary."[43]

It is notable in this context that Augustine is the most-cited saint in the *Catechism of the Catholic Church*: he is referenced eighty-five times. For comparison, the four female Doctors of the Church receive fourteen mentions, combined. Unsurprisingly, Ávila's frank assessment is not one of the spiritual gems that made it into the *Catechism*.

Beyond the *Catechism*, studies show that female figures are excluded from the consciousness of the church in ways that further subjugate women in Christianity.[44] For example, Mary Magdalene's role as a disciple and preacher of the divinity of Christ and the resurrection has been minimized in Scripture, and recent research indicates that the (male) writers and compilers of Gospel narratives sought to diminish her import by attributing some of her words and actions to other figures;[45] the status of Deacon Phoebe, St. Paul's trusted cohort, is often overlooked;[46] and the lectionary diminishes the crucial actions of Shiphrah and Puah—Hebrew midwives who defied Pharoah to deliver baby boys, including Moses—by cutting out their role in the story when proclaiming that piece of salvation history.[47]

Recognizing that we receive our faith tradition through a lens that prioritizes maleness (and in the United States at least, whiteness) is an important step toward conceiving of right relationships that do not depend on structures of domination—relationships that respond to Christ's call to oneness. Ivone Gebara—a Brazilian ecofeminist of the Sisters of Saint Augustine,

41. Gilligan, *Deepening Darkness*, 116.
42. Teresa of Ávila, *Way of Perfection*, Chapter 3.
43. Williams, *Subversive Habits*, 12.
44. See Ferris, "Bible on Steroids"; and Henderson, *Remembering the Women*.
45. See Schrader and Taylor, "Meaning of 'Magdalene.'"
46. See Peppard, "Household Names."
47. See Kelly, "Untold Stories."

who was censured by the Vatican in the late twentieth century[48]—recognizes the issue and suggests a cause: "In our patriarchal culture, where the consequences of colonialist slavery are still present, power is a men's issue, especially public power; because of this, God, considered as a super power, has a masculine face. In this cultural context of masculine and white domination, in Christian churches, feminism and ecofeminism are not well known and are sometimes considered a kind of heresy disturbing the community."[49]

Indeed, the hierarchical model of church relations lends itself to this power struggle. If human beings are driven by a lust for domination, structures of hierarchy will only exacerbate this sinful tendency. "When culture is based on a dominator model," observes bell hooks, "not only will it be violent, but it will frame all relationships as power struggles."[50] Because we have inherited a hierarchical, patriarchal worldview, prophetic female voices make us nervous, and questions are perceived as contradictions or challenges to our faith rather than legitimate interpretive efforts.

And this is not something that will just go away, even as women and people of color embody roles with more authority. It pains me to confess that up until I entered graduate school, I was reluctant to endorse the possibility of a female president because I had internalized the idea that women are too emotional to hold so much power. And as I write this chapter, news is breaking of a female member of the US House of Representatives issuing this statement on what it means to be a woman: "We came from Adam's rib. God created us with his hands. We may be the weaker sex, we are the weaker sex, but we are our partner's, our husband's wife."[51] Insofar as women, too, have been formed according to the same paradigm of static hierarchy and male dominance as that which informed Augustine's views and has been passed down through our church and culture, we cannot expect to break the habits of misogyny, racism, and androcentrism.

---

48. As the *National Catholic Reporter* (NCR) detailed at the time, "Gebara's silencing comes in the aftermath of comments she made on abortion in 1993 to a reporter from the Brazilian weekly Veja. The publication quoted her as saying abortion is not necessarily a sin for a poor woman psychologically incapable of confronting pregnancy. In a written defense in Brazil, Gebara responded: 'For me, as a Christian, to defend the decriminalization and legal regulation of abortion is not to deny the traditional teachings of the gospel of Jesus and the church. Rather, it is to welcome them within the paradoxical reality of human history and to aid in diminishing violence against life.' She signed another document confirming her defense of life in all its forms. The Vatican opted to silence her, claiming her theology was problematic" (Editors of *National Catholic Reporeter*, "Ivone Gebara").

49. Gebara, "Ecofeminism," 93.

50. hooks, *Will to Change*, 116.

51. See Muzaffar, "Marjorie Taylor Greene Mocked."

Indeed, Williams recalls "the distinguished theologian and nun who, in 2011, told me in a room full of scholars and lay people that there were 'anthropological' reasons why white nuns did not want to live with Black women and girls called to consecrated life. This was after she begrudgingly acknowledged the history of racial segregation and anti-Black exclusion in women's religious life."[52] And I suspect many readers may have experienced their own suffering of various degrees at the hands of women religious themselves, especially prior to Vatican II reforms.

Though we might vigorously condemn previous atrocities, we also have to reckon with their ongoing implications. And if we do not correct the underlying framework that made it possible to sanction them, the application of our theology always will continue to sanction new kinds of injustice. As Robin Wall Kimmerer reminds us, "cosmologies are a source of identity and orientation to the world. They tell us who we are. We are inevitably shaped by them no matter how distant they are from our consciousness."[53]

AN EVOLVING TRADITION

Perhaps the realization that the disorder of Augustine's intellectual paradigm has contributed to so much violence should have prompted me to abandon my efforts to internalize his theology and spirituality in my personal life; perhaps it should have made me reticent to implement his thought in my work for peace and justice. But after journeying with him for so many years, I could no more do that than turn away from the Catholic tradition itself. And it was clear to me that if hierarchy is problematic because it entices the *libido dominandi*, Augustine himself offers compelling reasons to dismantle it. Indeed, I found that the new insights I was exploring with the SSND were not actually "new," as much as reimagined. In Augustine, I found these insights richly articulated—provided I read him with a different lens.

Augustine, too, reflects on the need for our spiritual sensibilities to evolve. "Justice," he writes, "contains in itself at one and the same time all the principles which it prescribes, without discrepancy; although, as times change, it prescribes and apportions them, not all at once, but according to the needs of the times."[54] In other words, allowing our norms and customs to change is a healthy expression of faith that recognizes its limits, provided our new ways of being fit with the justice that is the eternal law, the right order of the whole. Consciousness evolving is a sign of the Spirit at work.

52. Williams, "I Wrote the First Full History."
53. Kimmerer, *Braiding Sweetgrass*, 7.
54. Augustine, *Confessions*, III.7.

Although Augustine compares God to a king issuing decrees, "for all must yield to God just as, in the government of human society, the lesser authority must yield to the greater,"[55] his emphasis on the movement of all of creation toward God can help to rearticulate this hierarchical language. Indeed, Augustine laments the human desire to have the questions of our moral lives settled, once and for all, as though the dictates we discern are absolute. He writes, "This is what happens, O Fountain of Life, when we abandon you, who are the Creator of all that ever was or is, and each of us proudly sets his heart on some one part of your creation instead of on the whole."[56] We need not think of God as an arbitrary ruler, but we can yield to the pull of the Spirit who moves our hearts toward wholeness, through love. Is this not just another way to speak of conversion, of turning our limited vision toward the whole?

Augustine is convinced that "many of the things we do may therefore seem wrong to men but are approved in the light of your knowledge, and many which men applaud are condemned in your eyes."[57] And he is not speaking, here, of non-Christian men, as though Christians possess the full wisdom to determine what is approved by divine knowledge; rather, his assessment applies to all human beings—Christian and secular, alike. Augustine calls for modest moral convictions, and even his most aggressively articulated assertions are qualified by his acknowledgment of personal fallibility—though this might seem poor consolation to many of us, the modern heirs of some of his more problematic claims.

For Augustine, there are some sins that are to be condemned always and everywhere because they are sins against nature, reflecting a desire to usurp the role of Creator by contradicting God's plan for creation. But it is an open question whether our evolving awareness of the natural world would have moved Augustine to modify his list of sins falling into that category. He recognizes that "God gave [people in the past] one commandment and has given us another. He has done this because the times have demanded it, although men were subjected to the same justice in those days as we are in these."[58] And if the command is always to increase relationship—to affirm interconnection, to "be one"—then sins against nature would be those that foment division. The way we interpret natural law itself should reflect an evolutive, open posture. "This does not mean that justice is erratic or variable, but that the times over which it presides are not always the same,"

55. Augustine, *Confessions*, III.8.

56. Augustine, *Confessions*, III.8.

57. Augustine, *Confessions*, III.9.

58. Augustine, *Confessions*, III.7.

Augustine assures us, "for it is the nature of time to change."[59] What we consider to be just, or right, should evolve as our consciousness evolves.

Observing that humans tend to judge others based on their own cultural customs, rather than appreciating the diverse movement of the Spirit, Augustine uses a litany of analogies to show the ignorance of such a position. For example, he compares those who think their own customs are always and everywhere just to "a man who knows nothing about armour and cannot tell which piece is meant for which part of the body, so that he tries to cover his head with a shin-piece and fix a helmet on his foot, and then complains because they will not fit."[60] At the same time, he rejects individualistic tendencies to determine what is good for ourselves, by ourselves, without reference to a broader tradition or a community of faith. This too, he thinks, reflects ignorance and self-aggrandizement.

Indeed, Augustine recognizes the strong grip cultural and personal habits have on the moral vision of men, though I think his insights apply equally well to those of us of other genders:

> Man's life on earth is short and he cannot, by his own perception, see the connexion [sic] between the conditions of earlier times and of other nations, which he has not experienced himself, and those of his own times, which are familiar to him. But when only one individual, one day, or one house is concerned, he can easily see what is suitable for each part of the whole and for each member of the household, and what must be done at which times and places.[61]

In other words, human beings struggle to recognize unity in difference, so we assume differences run counter to truth, rather than appreciating them as diverse expressions of the whole.

Our limited vision cannot comprehend the scope of the whole, but as we make our way through life, we want the assurance that we are living well. This is perhaps why our culture wars have reached a breaking point. We are living at the precipice of a new era. There is an "overarching backdrop of conflict," Pat Farrell, OSF, writes, "reflected [in] the breaking down of one era and the emergence of another. We [are] living a tug-of-war between the desire to preserve long-held values, traditions, and institutions and the impulse to reach toward emerging alternatives."[62] Unable to rest with the uncertainty of the moral life, we assert our own sense of the good as absolute.

59. Augustine, *Confessions*, III.7.
60. Augustine, *Confessions*, III.7.
61. Augustine, *Confessions*, III.7.
62. Farrell, "Tapestry of Contrasting Colors," in Sanders, *However Long the Night*, 85.

The cosmology of hierarchy that maintains a static order of truth normalizes dominance and frames relationships in terms of power dynamics, playing right into our *libido dominandi*. We forget that the tug of war between preservation and progress need not entail the dominance of one side or the other. We do not need to reject tradition because we have acknowledged its shortcomings—rather, we can mine tradition to discover new interpretations that avoid past pitfalls, carrying through the good of what has been into the good that is becoming. Indeed, it is the cosmology of hierarchy that makes us perceive challenges and questions as power grabs, rather than as legitimate opportunities for dialogue and growth. But theology is not about power; it is about love.

RETHINKING ORDER

Given the dangers posed by a worldview premised on hierarchy as a model of power relations, it is at least worth considering whether a new paradigm could better express our Christian faith. Most of us, I think, recognize the many sins committed by the church in the pursuit of power. Fewer of us, perhaps, are willing to question the paradigm that motivates them. But question it we must.

Rosemary Radford Ruether, referencing Gebara, puts the point more strongly: we must "dismantle the whole paradigm of male over female, mind over body, heaven over earth, transcendent over immanent, the male God outside of and ruling over the created world—and . . . imagine an alternative to it."[63] And Ganim, reflecting on the hierarchical model of community that sanctioned male superiority in her religious order, puts it thus:

> We believe that those of us who were and are out of order were harbingers of these ideas and changes within both church and society. Our task has been to work the metaphor, to help our sisters and our brothers within the church and in our workplaces and neighborhoods and communities to understand the constraints of too much order. We are pushing the metaphor of being out of order as a way of saying that the former constructs of religious life and the role of women in the Catholic Church are outmoded, that being out of the old order is good, and that a newer order of life based on openness, love, and justice is the order of tomorrow.[64]

63. Ruether, "Ecofeminist Philosophy," in Kearns and Keller, *Ecospirit*, 85.
64. Ganim, "Unruly Women," in DelRosso, *Unruly Catholic Nuns*, 59.

An ethic of right order that moves us toward right relationships is compelling, but if we get the order wrong, the consequences are disastrous.

If, as Augustine recognizes, sin inheres in the human will to dominate, rather than to abide in solidarity, a worldview premised on exclusion and hierarchy will lend itself to the perpetration of injustice. Despite the important insight that rightly ordered love fosters justice as right relationship, it is irresponsible and dangerous to ignore the harms motivated by order arranged according to the dominative hierarchical model. Reorganizing Augustine's ethic according to new cosmology can help us to interpret our faith tradition in a more holistic way. As Augustine knew, the love that moves us cannot be ordered rightly unless it manifests in right relationships; but relationships premised on static hierarchy cannot be right.

Importantly, "new" is perhaps the wrong descriptor for the paradigm of interconnection that will be explored in what follows. As Johnson observes, "such an alternative [paradigm] presents itself in the biblical view of the community of creation. Widespread in prophets, psalms, and wisdom writings, this paradigm positions humans not above but within the living world which has its own relationship to God accompanied by a divinely-given mandate to thrive."[65]

As the hierarchical paradigm has become more prevalent in Western society, this insight has fallen out of Catholic consciousness, though it has been embodied in the wisdom of marginalized traditions and confirmed through scientific discoveries. As Miles recognizes,

> Having been treated as possessions and deprived of ownership of themselves, their families, crops they nurtured, and objects they made and maintained, African American survivors of slavery recognized the world of things. They lived each day in haunted awareness of the thin boundary line between human and non-human, a thinness daily exposed and abused by slave societies. Despite the prominence of a Cartesian duality in Western philosophy that proposed a clear split between spirit and matter, enslaved Blacks knew that people could be treated like things and things prized over people. Awash in this awful knowledge, African Americans may have been early theorists of the mercurial nature of things. In this understanding, they would have joined Native Americans, the first thing-thinkers on this continent who affirmed in their stories and lived through their actions a belief that many things have a kind of spirit and are capable of relationship. In their everyday lives, Indigenous North Americans recognized the animated nature of things as

65. Johnson, *Ask the Beasts*, 267.

well as the innate relationality of people, non-human animals, and plants, all of which, scientists now confirm, share common fundamental elements (such as cell structure, chemical makeup, and DNA).[66]

If we attend to the wisdom of marginalized communities, we learn that interconnection is the basis of all life—"including that life considered un-alive by Euro-science: rocks, rivers, lakes, mountains and the like."[67]

Riane Eisler has demonstrated that the dominator model of society "which has prevailed over most of recorded history, is a patriarchal or androcratic social structure based on the ranking of men over women in a domination hierarchy ultimately backed up by force or the threat of force."[68] This stands in contrast to partnership models, present especially in primitive and Indigenous cultures, which are ways "of structuring human relations—be they of men and women, or of different races, religions, and nations—in which diversity is not automatically equated with inferiority or superiority" and the "organizational principle . . . is linking," rather than ranking.[69] She highlights the incongruity:

> The Judaeo-Christian Bible tells of a garden where woman and man lived in harmony with each other and nature—a time before a male god decreed that woman henceforth be subservient to man.[70] . . . As we enter recorded history we begin to see oscillations between periods of partnership resurgence followed, until now, by periods of regression toward a more faithful approximation of the androcratic model—for example, the rise of early Christianity inspired by the partnership teachings of Jesus, followed by the rigidly male-dominant, authoritarian, and highly violent (as in its inquisitions and witchburnings) "orthodox" Church.[71]

Interpreting our faith through the lens of Christ's call to oneness, then, enfolds what has been into what is emerging, taking us back to our origins as we move forward in hope.

"The great challenge," Gebara summarizes, "is whether Christianity will be flexible enough to change the foundations of its anthropology and

---

66. Miles, *All That She Carried*, 268.
67. Kidwell et al., *Native American Theology*, 81.
68. Eisler, "Dynamics," 161.
69. Eisler, "Dynamics," 161.
70. Eisler, "Dynamics," 163.
71. Eisler, "Dynamics," 167.

cosmology,"[72] or perhaps we could say—to reimagine them. Like her, "I think it can. And I think it must."[73]

Ironically, because Augustine identifies God as the One, through whom rightly ordered love facilitates unity in right relationship, his theological vision offers a particularly helpful way to do so. Although he maintains the hierarchical language of "ascent" to oneness, we can reconstruct the themes his account contains and use the framework to promote encounter, instead. As Judith Chelius Stark recognizes, "embedded in the life of the divine trinity and in the inner life of the mind in which Augustine discovers and enunciates the divine image in humans, are the principles of equality, reciprocity, mutuality, and interrelationship. Both the life of God and the inner life of humans have these qualities as constitutive of their very essence. . . . Hierarchy or rigid subordination [do not] enter into his thinking on these points. In these ways," she argues, Augustine's theological insights "may come to serve wider purposes of inclusion and correcting his 'malecentered spiritualism.'"[74]

When we adjust Augustine's cosmology of hierarchy, these principles of his thought can be extended through the whole of his account and a new ethic can emerge—indeed, it is emerging through the SSND community and other communities of women religious. And so, as Stark tells us, "We are left to imagine and to work out what might have happened had Augustine drawn out the implications of his own paradigm of interrelationship, based on equality, mutuality, and reciprocity, that he discovered as the inner life of God."[75]

I confess that before I met the sisters, I was resistant to such reimagining and associated cosmological language with new-age spirituality that ran afoul of orthodoxy. My views paralleled those of Ann Carey, for example, who registers her disdain for women religious embracing new cosmology by reminding us that the Bishops have censured many women for writing and speaking in cosmological terms. "Surely such New-Age theories," she writes, "pale in comparison to the rich deposit of the faith in sacred Scripture and Tradition entrusted to the teaching office of the Catholic Church."[76]

However, both Scripture and tradition make it quite clear that our faith is one of creativity and radical unity, though they have been interpreted, at times, in ways that are stilted and divisive. It is a gift of the Spirit

72. Ress, "Interview," 110.

73. Ress, "Interview," 110.

74. Stark, "Augustine on Women," in Stark, *Feminist Interpretations*, 237.

75. Stark, "Augustine on Women," in Stark, *Feminist Interpretations*, 238.

76. Carey, "Women Religious."

that although sacred Scripture and tradition are rooted in the "old" cosmology of hierarchy, they nevertheless hold the basis for new cosmology. Reinterpreting our faith in light of new awareness, then, need not occur "in comparison" to the teaching office, but in tandem with it.

The *Catechism* tells us that although human reason can attain to God, our language never can capture fully the ultimate mystery of the divine. The authors refer to God in masculine terms throughout the document, but they nevertheless instruct us to "continually purify our language of everything in it that is limited, image-bound, or imperfect, if we are not to confuse our image of God . . . with our human representations."[77] It is at least possible that in interpreting the tenets of our faith, the hierarchy has been limited in its discernment. As I watched the sisters live out the call to oneness, I began to suspect that the exclusion of female voices might have had an inhibitive effect on the Catholic tradition and, at the very least, it is worth considering whether their insights could teach us anything about our faith.

And so I began to absorb the wisdom of these women, who dedicate their lives to Christ and open their spirits to Jesus's desire that "all may be one." As I reflected on their emerging consciousness, I realized that the insights they offer are not at odds with the central tenets of our faith, as I had once thought. Rather, they open new horizons and enrich our way of seeing the world that can fill in gaps and bridge divides that mark our church today.

I used to ask, as Carey does, when the church's "message [will be] heard and accepted by the new cosmologists who claim that they are also Catholic?"[78] But perhaps these are better questions: Why do we so often admire the ministry of women religious but question the faith that motivates them if it offers new or underappreciated interpretations of our tradition? And if our faith tradition has been influenced by an incorrect notion of the cosmos, why should we resist those who try to reimagine what it means to be Catholic according to a more accurate cosmology?

Our faith tradition is indeed rich, and by reckoning with the harmful aspects of its distorted cosmology, we can begin to enjoy its richness in more holistic ways. New cosmology can enhance, rather than erode, the Catholic tradition by enfolding the core of our faith—the call to oneness in Christ—within a paradigm that recognizes interconnection, not hierarchy, as the fundamental descriptor of cosmic order.

77. Catechism of the Catholic Church (hereafter CCC) I.1.IV.42.
78. Carey, "Women Religious."

PAUSE FOR REFLECTION

Take a moment to reflect on what you read.

- What is drawing your attention? What words, phrases, or concepts stand out to you? Are any new insights stirring in you?
- Where do you sense the most resistance to new awareness in your consciousness? What limits have constrained your moral vision?
- What do you make of the distinction between bringing Christ to others versus seeing Christ in others?

3

Discovering Our Place in the Cosmos

An Imaginative Conversion

We are yet in the presence of the strange form of grace even cynics call love.

—Louise Erdrich, *Shadow Tag*

IF HUMAN BEINGS ARE concerned with power, we are suspicious of vulner-ability. Our hearts of stone guard against change;[1] we pretend to isolate reason from experience so we can maintain a sense of certitude as we keep our spheres of influence neatly ordered. But isn't imagination the ability to peer beyond our known boundaries in delight and expectation? Static hierarchy tells us that there is nothing beyond these boundaries; hope tells us otherwise.

To offer hope, however, faithful imagination must resonate with ex-perience and knowledge—it must incorporate what we know but draw us toward new meanings. Augustine knew this too. As Todd Breyfogle explains, "Augustine's account cannot abide Romanticism's understanding

1. Ezek 36:26.

58

(now dominant) of imagination as subjective artistic invention. Even at its highest power, imagination remains the discovery of objective reality and is never an autonomous creativity (which only God can possess)."[2] The Catholic imagination is known for its iconic and sacramental imagery—for appreciating metaphor and finding God present in all things. But if our Catholic imagination is to remain significant, it should reflect the empirical reality in which we find ourselves. Religious imagination must be grounded in reality, or it is merely fantasy.

This year, my children were studying ancient history with their home-school co-op, and one of their first assignments was to read the creation story in Genesis 1. Though they know the story by heart, we read it again, and they obligingly colored the corresponding pictures. To supplement this lesson, I also read them a gorgeously illustrated picture book about the origins and evolution of the universe, according to the latest scientific discoveries. As I began the first page, my first grader looked up from his coloring with eyes wide, mouth agape, crayon frozen in air. By the second page, he had put aside his worksheet and moved closer for a better view. "Is this real, Mommy?" he asked intently. When I answered affirmatively, he gasped and remained transfixed for the remainder of the book. As we read, he delighted in discovering every piece of the biblical creation myth enfolded in the empirical account.

With the perceptive insight of a child, my son recognized intuitively that the reality of evolution in the cosmos displayed truth and beauty that the Genesis story, when taken literally, had stopped short of conveying to him. Though he welcomed the opportunity to think about what the Scriptures reveal to help us understand the cosmos and our place in it, he was captivated by the mystery and beauty of immanent reality, which opens a pathway to transcendent possibilities. That, to me, is the gift of cosmological consciousness: it expands our imaginations.

Beauty always draws us beyond ourselves; it takes us by surprise and dehabituates us from the tedium of our preconceived reality, and from the consuming appetites that drive us to exaggerate created goods beyond their limits.[3] When we encounter the beautiful, we experience the delight of si-multaneous resonance and otherness: we find we belong, and yet we are in the presence of mystery.

To situate ourselves within that space is to grapple with our limitations in light of a seemingly infinite expanse. The cosmological spirituality emerg-ing in many women religious invites imagination as it evolves tradition, and

2. Breyfogle, "Imagination," in Fitzgerald, *Augustine through the Ages.*
3. I am indebted to Jim Wetzel on this point.

it is for this reason, perhaps even more than its empirical accuracy, that it is critically important to life today.

Toward the end of the narrative chapters of his *Confessions*, Augustine describes a similar epiphany during a mystical vision with his mother, Monica. He recalls being caught up in delightful conversation that led the two of them, together, beyond the beauty of individual beings to the contemplation of their source:

> As the flame of love burned stronger in us and raised us higher towards the eternal God our thoughts ranged over the whole compass of material things in their various degrees, up to the heavens themselves, from which the sun and the moon and the stars shine down upon the earth. Higher still we climbed, thinking and speaking all the while in wonder at all that you have made. At length we came to our own souls and passed beyond them to that place of everlasting plenty.[4]

In that moment, Augustine imagines all of creation falling silent, foregoing its limited expression of being in joint contemplation of the wholeness of being itself. Augustine feels his integral connection with the entire community of creation, and he is overwhelmed by the peace that inheres as all, together, attend to the whole.[5]

EMERGING COSMOLOGY

The way we understand the cosmos has profound implications for understanding ourselves in relation to the whole of creation, and our evolving understanding of the cosmos offers insights into theological reflection. While Western ancient and medieval cosmologies asserted a static hierarchy of being, we know now that the cosmos has been expanding and evolving, building on simple organisms to form more complex entities. As Delio emphasizes, "We simply do not live in a static, fixed cosmos."[6]

From the beginning of time, creation has been energized to develop more diverse forms of being and to form increasingly complex relationships. Reflecting the Creator, a Trinity who exists as relationship, the universe evolves through relationships, toward oneness, or wholeness. "The Universe Story," Judy Cannato writes, "besides telling us that we are part of a single creation event, is an evolutionary one . . . a dynamic process at the

---

4. Augustine, *Confessions*, IX.10.

5. This point was sharpened in conversation with Erika Kidd and Veronica Ogle.

6. Delio, *Making All Things New*, 79.

heart of the created world, characterized by increased diversity with greater, more complex consciousness."[7] Cannato explains:

> Prior to the discovery of quantum mechanics, Newtonian phys-
> ics asserted that the atom, a word which means "indivisible,"
> was the fundamental unit of matter. Scientists thought they
> had reached the bottom line of the material world and could
> therefore explain reality on that basis. But quantum physics
> turned that notion upside-down, demonstrating that atoms are
> not hard-boundaried units and that there is an entire world of
> sub-atomic particles that can be described as either particles
> or waves. And what scientists are now saying is that if we look
> down farther and farther, on smaller and smaller scales, what
> we come to is not some "thing," but something like information,
> thought, or consciousness.[8]

The implications of this quantum perspective are vast. Note, for example, that the understanding of the material world has shifted from one of auton-omous independence and hard boundaries to one of interbeing—of active relationality that constitutes reality. Note also that even matters considered settled must be reexamined when new information or experiences chal-lenge our preconceived convictions.

Delio emphasizes this point, as well, writing that "whereas Newton thought the material universe was made of inert matter, we now know that the material universe is fundamentally energy."[9] Through quantum cosmology, Catherine Keller explains, "we are learning of an immediate connectivity operating across the widest distances, where there is no empty void but rather an infinitely plastic body of mysterious energy. And the very energy of the expansion may flow from the intimacy of the entanglement."[10] We live in a universe whose foundation is energy directed toward relation-ship—energy that expands outward only through the entangled being, the intimate relationships, of its parts. Keller adds encouragingly: "Never mind the math. Consider the metaphor!"[11]

All matter from the beginning of time has been expanding and making new connections, and that very act of relating constitutes the core of being itself. Is this not an image of the trinitarian principle of unity-in-diversity?

7. Cannato, *Field of Compassion*, 21.

8. Cannato, *Field of Compassion*, 9.

9. Delio, *Making All Things New*, 38.

10. Keller, "Energy We Are," in Bowman and Crockett, *Cosmology*, 23.

11. Keller, "Energy We Are," in Bowman and Crockett, *Cosmology*, 23.

The cosmos—the whole—is made up of the relationships among smaller wholes, which in turn are made up of even smaller wholes. Scientists call these *holons*. Referring to Arthur Koestler's work in the 1960s, Cannato explains that "in essence, the theory of holons states that everything in the universe is a whole-part. Nothing is whole apart from everything else, and nothing is a part separate from other wholes."[12] Here, there is surely resonance with Augustine's part/whole analysis of the cosmos, which leads him to reprove "any part that is out of keeping with the whole."[13] However, while his understanding of the whole was organized by static hierarchy, contemporary observations indicate that the whole exists as evolutive interconnection.

Cannato describes the concept of *holons* with the image "of nesting dolls—one inside the other, inside the other, inside the other. A cell is nested in the molecule, the molecule is nested in the atom. This holds true for every level of complexity and demonstrates how all life is connected, with each stage of development emerging out of the one before it."[14] And because this whole/part awareness applies to the entire cosmos, we are, with physicist David Bohm, "looking at the universe in terms of a new order."[15]

Bohm puts this in terms of "the *enfolded order* or the *implicate order*."[16] The implicate order, Heidi Russell explains, is "the whole of the universe actively folded into each part, and that enfoldment is different in each part and is central to determining what each part *is*."[17] We are constituted by our relationships, but not in a way that objectifies our existence as inferior or superior to others; rather, in a way that connects us in the ever more expansive consciousness contained in the whole of being. In other words, the fundamental order of the universe is not one of hierarchy, but one of interconnection.

This is reflected in Bohm's claim that "there is one energy that is the basis of all reality."[18] Everything is connected. And as Delio has suggested, "the quantum vacuum can be seen as a modern scientific understanding of what Saint Augustine called the *rationes seminales*, a doctrine whereby all the seeds of creation (the potential powers of everything that could be) were given in the first instance of creation. Similarly, the quantum vacuum means

12. Cannato, *Field of Compassion*, 32.
13. Augustine, *Confessions*, III.8.
14. Augustine, *Confessions*, III.8.
15. Bohm, *Unfolding Meaning*, 12.
16. Bohm, *Unfolding Meaning*, 12.
17. Russell, *Source of All Love*, 16.
18. Quoted in Zohar, *Quantum Self*, 58.

that everything, including consciousness, is present in the big bang."[19] As the universe evolves and expands, it is pulled toward wholeness, inclusive of all that is, has been, and ever will be.

Cannato recognizes the implications of this: "Emerging from a single quantum vacuum," she writes, "it seems that we remain connected through-out our lives, bound together by a mysterious energy that makes all creation a single whole."[20] In other words, all of creation is moving with the energy of being toward the wholeness that includes all consciousness, relationships, and matter—a wholeness that is not static because it is, itself, relational energy. This concept of energy in relationship is critical for thinking about God, who is trinity, who is love.

Indeed, Russell recognizes that "love is a particularly appropriate title for God because it can function as both subject and verb. One can address God as love, and the title is both personal and descriptive."[21] Rather than conjuring visions of a humanesque God, the language of love draws us to-ward our relational essence and offers a way of relating to the whole beyond our limited selves. As Russell explains,

> Our language is structured in such a way as to reinforce our understanding of ourselves as separate individuals rather than reinforcing the ways in which we are interconnected. This false fragmentation is particularly important in the way it distorts our understanding of God. God is understood as another individual alongside us who acts in the world as we do, albeit on a grander scale. For example, to say that God loves or God loves us implies a false distinction between God and love. One might say, "Love loves." Likewise, when this same grammatical structure of our language is applied to the Trinity, we end up talking about the Three as three individuals. The Trinity is not three subjects who relate to one another, but rather God is relation or relating.[22]

When we reimagine God as the loving energy that forms matter and draws it toward wholeness through the development of new relationships, the problematic vertical and horizontal dichotomy disappears.

God is both present in material evolution and is the wholeness *beyond*, not above, the experience of being a limited body. As we forge new relationships and expand our consciousness, keeping our eyes fixed on the dynamic

---

19. Delio, *Making All Things New*, 58.
20. Cannato, *Field of Compassion*, 19.
21. Russell, *Source of All Love*, 27.
22. Russell, *Source of All Love*, 27.

wholeness of being, we act in ways that reflect the image of God—the whole of all that is, the love that moves us.

Augustine, too, recognizes that the word of God is "not speech in which each part comes to an end when it has been spoken, giving place to the next, so that finally the whole may be uttered. In your word," Augustine writes, "all is uttered at one and the same time, yet eternally."[23] The whole—the word of God, wisdom, unity—is present in each speck of dust, in each new relationship; and yet, the whole transcends the limits of time and space. In evolution, "the beauty of the ages is unfolded in the coming and passing of things"[24] as each creature furthers the progress of creation toward its destiny: the absolute wholeness of being.

We limited creatures hold the whole within us and are moved by love to further wholeness through our engagement with the world. Keller writes, "In this vision the divine that serves as a lure to the process of evolution and complexification is a manifestation of cosmic desire. And inasmuch as we earthlings, on our way from dust to dust, meet that lure with delight, we release a fresh energy of symbiotic creativity. The throbbing eco-process universe brings us back, and then takes us forward to . . . quantum cosmology."[25] Keller recognizes that "we feel, amid our weirdness and our woes, the throb of eternal delight. We feel the energy we are."[26] Might this be the restlessness Augustine describes so poignantly in his *Confessions*? Our very being pulsates with the energy of the whole, and we find rest only when we accept the limits of our finitude and recognize ourselves—and all other beings—as enfolded together in love, the wholeness of being.

Johnson helpfully identifies the web of relationships on a more macro-scale: "If evolutionary science has established any great insight," she writes, "it is that all life on this planet forms one community. Historically, all life results from the same biological process; genetically, living beings share elements of the same basic code; functionally, species interact without ceasing."[27] Peace is not attached to a supernatural, static essence; rather, it is found through the transcendent grace that invites us into the web of relationships that constitutes the whole.

The interconnectedness of the cosmos means that our selves are constituted in part by other beings, so if Augustine is right, and the pursuit of God begins with introspective awareness, then God can only be found

23. Augustine, *Confessions*, XI.7.

24. Augustine, "On the Literal Interpretation," 1.8.14, in Augustine, *On Genesis*.

25. Keller, "Energy We Are," in Bowman and Crockett, *Cosmology*, 20.

26. Keller, "Energy We Are," in Bowman and Crockett, *Cosmology*, 25.

27. Johnson, *Ask the Beasts*, 267.

through authentic relationality as we seek ever expansive encounters. Renée Kohler-Ryan has recognized that Augustine does maintain a sense of a "metaphysically porous" self, arguing that "the interior needs to move from and through the exterior—pulling together body and soul—so as to stretch out as far as possible, with others and through creation, toward God."[28] In this, she observes, "A cosmic sense of personal identity thus opens up—the more one finds God in the world, the more one knows oneself."[29] We can see, here, that the cosmological awareness available to us today serves to undergird Augustine's sensibility of the self as relational.

Since we are discovering that consciousness is at the heart of matter, however, it no longer makes sense to seek God via the transcendence of matter. In fact, our pursuit of God—insofar as it involves tapping into consciousness of the ever-evolving whole—can occur only through fuller participation in the material world. As Delio writes, "Because our consciousness has emerged from this wholeness and continues to be part of it, then what accounts for the human mind is active in the universe."[30] In other words, mind and matter are not separate realms of being, but are interconnected.

Augustine's own trinitarian image of selfhood necessitates this inward/outward compatibility: insofar as each part of the Trinity constitutes and is constituted by the others, God is the interplay of whole beings forming a perfect whole, which pours out of itself in creative love. This is how we should view ourselves, and those we encounter in the cosmos. The human person cannot be known in isolation—and neither can the fullness of the Spirit. Rather, reality is constituted by relationship.

As we begin to recognize our interconnection, we increase our ability to see ourselves and our world holistically—to attain the vision of the One who Is,[31] the whole of all actualities and potentialities. "There is," Delio explains, "a single 'mysterious divinity' moving in the world, liberating unsuspected powers, promising and delivering more being, more unity, and more freedom. It is God active in creation, embodied in the universe."[32]

"And so," Gebara avers, "we are beginning to discover our interconnectedness. We humans are not 'Lords of creation.' Instead, we are the earth's thought, the earth's reflection of itself; one type of consciousness present on

28. Kohler-Ryan, "Augustine Pulling and Stretching," in Camacho and Clausen, *Studia Patristica*, 14.

29. Kohler-Ryan, "Augustine Pulling and Stretching," in Camacho and Clausen, *Studia Patristica*, 17.

30. Delio, *Making All Things New*, 62.

31. Augustine, *Confessions*, VII.17.

32. Delio, *Making All Things New*, 96.

the planet. We sense that all is in evolution, all is in all."[33] Since the dawn of time, the universe has moved energetically toward increasing connectivity and consciousness. The order of the cosmos is not one of hierarchy, but of expansive interconnection, and as we form new relationships, new ways of being emerge. "The Christian story," Cannato emphasizes, "has named that which brings about and maintains this creative process 'God.'"[34]

A GRAND TAPESTRY

In an essay entitled, "I Am a Catholic Nun," which appears in the intriguingly titled collection *Unruly Catholic Nuns: Sister Stories*, Sharon Kanis, SSND, recalls an epiphany:

> One day when I was walking alone, I had a profound experience that was for me like wandering into a parable: I saw an old woman sitting at a loom, weaving with silver threads. She was beautiful and vibrant and wore a simple brown robe. She said, "Don't worry. I am here and my work is being done. Let the powers do as they must." By this, I understood her to mean global, political, church, and community leaders who sometimes act in contradiction to God's desires. She continued, "I am very busy and my work is being done. I am connecting you to one another." Then I saw the people of the world connected through their hearts by a fine silver thread. I realized that the thread she was weaving to connect us was her own silver hair. Now I know only one thing for certain: God is not as we think.[35]

God the weaver is found in Scripture, too. The psalmist, for example, marvels that God "knit me together in my mother's womb."[36] Though the focus of this passage in contemporary discourse often turns toward the body in the womb, the image of God as weaver is profound.

Tiya Miles's book, *All That She Carried: The Journey of Ashley's Sack, a Black Family Keepsake*, contains a powerful historical narrative about the transcendent import of physical things, especially fabric. It focuses on the journey of a sack filled with essentials and love and given by Rose, an enslaved mother, to her daughter Ashley, who was trafficked away from her and then passed it down, along with the stories, through generations, until

---

33. Ress, "Interview," 112.

34. Cannato, *Field of Compassion*, 45.

35. Kanis, "I Am a Catholic Nun," in DelRosso, *Unruly Catholic Nuns*, 91.

36. Ps 139:13.

one granddaughter, Ruth, embroidered its history directly onto the bag in colorful thread. Miles writes,

> Fabric . . . stands out for its symbolic resonance in the history of African American women, enslaved or free, and women across boundaries of race and class. . . . As a pliable and fragile type of thing, fabric uniquely conveys psychic meanings. . . . The constituent parts of a textile—filaments woven, knitted, or fused—are countless elements made into one. Fabric therefore represents the connectedness of many threads that together create a whole cloth. It weakens over time through repeated use, washing, and sun exposure, lending it a quality of delicacy requiring care. Because of this innate multiplicity and natural fragility, cloth has stood for people across time and cultures. It symbolically represents our own bodies, our temporal lifelines, and our social ties to one another.[37]

And Miles draws this important connection: "Fabric is a special category of thing to people—damageable, weak at its edges, and yet life-sustaining. In these distinctive features, cloth begins to sound like this singular planet we call home."[38]

When we embrace our limits and relationality, we participate in the creative energy of God, imaging the inherently relational, creative, and life-sustaining Trinity by weaving our lives together with others' toward the flourishing of all. All of creation is intimately connected in an ever-evolving, ever-expanding universe. Finding God in that expanse is a lifelong pursuit; and yet, we ourselves embody it. In contemplating the beauty of the cosmos, we sense our smallness, and yet we know that we are part of a grand tapestry; we affirm our uniqueness, yet we recognize that our identity is defined in part by our participation in a larger project. We are *holons* becoming whole. And "all along the way of becoming," Laurie Brink, OP, reminds us, "God is urging, acting, inviting and loving us into this reconciled, emerging reality."[39]

So what does it mean for our moral lives if we identify God with wholeness, as the love that unifies and vivifies the threads of our collective being? In a reflection written for the SSND, Arlene Flaherty, OP, emphasizes,

> One-ness is the Divine design for life that calls forth from everyone a commitment to nurture and generate unity through our lives and mission. The diverse, fragile, yet generative web of life is created and sustained through right relationship, mutuality,

37. Miles, *All That She Carried*, 271.
38. Miles, *All That She Carried*, 272.
39. Brink, *Heavens Are Telling*, 180.

and cooperation among many varied life forms. These insights compel us to think anew about our commitment "to be one," with ourselves, each other, and with the earth.[40]

Acknowledging lack, embracing uncertainty, thinking anew, seeking expansive encounter—these are the features of cosmic spirituality.

PAUSE FOR REFLECTION

Take a moment to reflect on what you read.

- What is drawing your attention? What words, phrases, or concepts stand out to you? Are any new insights stirring in you?

- What does "cosmology" mean to you? Does it means something different now than when you started this chapter?

- *The diverse, fragile, yet generative web of life is created and sustained through right relationship, mutuality, and cooperation among many varied life forms.* What does this insight evoke in you?

40. Flaherty, "Introduction."

4

Enfolding Tradition with Evolving Consciousness

A Theological Conversion

There are many times when the idea that there is indeed a pattern
seems absurd wishful thinking. Random events abound. There
is much in life that seems meaningless. And then, when I can see
no evidence of meaning, some glimpse is given which reveals the
strange weaving of purposefulness and beauty. . . . I do not find it
any more difficult to live with the paradox of a universe of random-
ness and chance and a universe of pattern and purpose than I do
with light as a wave and light as a particle. Living with contradiction
is nothing new to the human being.

—MADELEINE L'ENGLE, *TWO-PART INVENTION*

CONTEMPLATING THE IMPLICATIONS OF this emergent vision of God for
our faith tradition can be daunting. Does understanding God as the energy
of creation, the love that draws us toward wholeness, really align with our
Catholic faith? I have found that the conversion of consciousness inspired

by this cosmology not only aligns with, but enriches my understanding of and appreciation for the Catholic tradition. Like my son's rapturous delight in the science of the universe, my spirit quickens as new discoveries resonate with my traditional sensibilities but pull me more deeply and creatively into theological exploration.

Consider the doctrines of original sin and the grace of Christ. What new insights can we gain into the origin of sin and its consequences? What can we discover about Christ in relation to the wholeness that we have broken, and which calls us to unity?

ORIGINAL SIN[1]

Reflecting on the fall in light of what we are learning about evolution and cosmology affirms the doctrine of original sin while offering new interpretations that can guide us today. Accepting the *Catechism*'s principle that "we cannot tamper with the revelation of original sin without undermining the mystery of Christ"[2] need not deter us from considering such revelation through the lens of cosmic interconnection.

In Genesis 3, Eve tells the serpent that God said of one tree in the garden, "You shall not eat it or even touch it, or else you will die." The snake replies, "You certainly will not die! God knows well that when you eat of it your eyes will be opened and you will be like gods, who know good and evil." On one reading of this story, we see a ruling God, issuing decrees that demand obedience on pain of death. But on a reading that imagines God as the wholeness of being, might we understand this dialogue as a warning of what was to come, rather than a divine decree?

I read the story of the fall as a reflection on the evolution of consciousness: prior to human beings, there was no moral awareness; everything existed in an evolutive cycle. Then human beings emerged from the earth, conscious of the wholeness of being yet sensing their own finitude. They became "like gods, who know good and evil." Incapable of expressing the fullness of love, but unwilling to abide limitations, human existence became a torturous effort to exceed them.

Perhaps our desire to dominate and control is the evolutionary residue of nonhuman ancestors who did not possess the capacity of consciousness to look at the world through a transcendent lens. The evolution of human beings with free will, who can *choose* whether to maintain a limited

1. The themes in this chapter were developed previously in Bonnette, "Habits of the Flesh."
2. CCC §389.

worldview or direct their gaze toward the whole, provides the occasion for sin. But if the dialogue between Eve and the Serpent was a foretelling, not a decree, then our focus on that story should shift to our original ancestors' attempts to grapple with their evolving moral consciousness.

Like the Whole, but Not Whole

In Augustine's account of the fall, we see two related, if distinct, motivations for sin. The first is the willingness to be deceived, which he attributes to Eve: "The woman accepted as true what the serpent told her."[3] But perhaps Eve's sin is rather that in eating the fruit, she took something that was not given to her. Departing from the truth of interconnected wholeness, Eve turned inward, prioritizing her own desires and giving in to the lust for domination, deceived by the thought that the world was hers for the taking.

Robin Wall Kimmerer interprets Eve's role in the fall from an Indigenous perspective, writing,

> On one side of the world were people whose relationship with the living world was shaped by Skywoman, who created a garden for the well-being of all. On the other side was another woman with a garden and a tree. But for tasting its fruit, she was banished from the garden and the gates clanged shut behind her. That mother of men was made to wander in the wilderness and earn her bread by the sweat of her brow, not by filling her mouth with the sweet juicy fruits that bend the branches low. In order to eat, she was instructed to subdue the wilderness into which she was cast. . . . Same species, same earth, different stories. . . . One story leads to the generous embrace of the living world, the other to banishment. One woman is our ancestral gardener, a cocreator of the good green world that would be the home of her descendants. The other was an exile, just passing through an alien world on a rough road to her real home in heaven.[4]

Certainly, the way we have interpreted the fall and the original paradise has lent itself to this analysis. But can we imagine the story afresh? Perhaps these stories are not so different, after all.

Kimmerer presents the precepts of the Indigenous instructions known as the Honorable Harvest: We are "to take only what is given, to use it well, to be grateful for the gift, and to reciprocate the gift."[5] In Eve's sin, we see

3. Augustine, *City of God*, XIV.11.

4. Kimmerer, *Braiding Sweetgrass*, 6.

5. Kimmerer, *Braiding Sweetgrass*, 21.

the taking of fruit that was not given, and we see her eat it out of a sense of entitlement, not gratitude. Perhaps the subsequent legacy of exile—the "bruises of an abusive relationship"[6] embodied by the brokenness of the land and its inhabitants—is precisely the consequence of failing to act on the awareness that "all flourishing is mutual";[7] failing to recognize that, as Pope Francis reminds us, "all creatures are connected [and] each must be cherished with love and respect, for all of us as living creatures are dependent on one another."[8]

So goes Eve's story. Adam's story follows a different path, as Augustine takes it. Augustine suggests that Adam ate the fruit offered by Eve because he "could not bear to be severed from his only companion, even though this involved a partnership in sin."[9] In other words, Adam was forced to choose between honoring God's commandment but losing his wife, or accompanying Eve into the abyss.

Augustine experiences the weight of a similarly impossible decision in his own journey. He, too, made a choice between the love of a woman, the mother of his child, and the pursuit of God. In some ways, his *Confessions* can be read as his attempt to heal his "bleeding heart" with the conviction that pursuing a higher good will be worth it—although his reflections often give the impression that after rejecting his love, he now feels anything but whole.[10]

Perhaps the emotionally raw Augustine found some salve by reading into the biblical narrative the seductive powers of women. How often have I myself lashed out at others to assuage my pain? Unfortunately for us, Augustine's misplaced accusations had more extensive ramifications than our typical emotional reactions, as we saw in chapter 2.

And yet—Augustine's struggles mimic, I think, those he identifies in Adam: When does love of a particular other inhibit our love of the whole? Augustine cannot bring himself to flip the query, perhaps because he feels it too deeply: When does love of the whole inhibit love of a particular other? He instead asserts that love of God frees human love to be authentic; and his point is well-taken: when we cling too tightly to our loves, we suffocate them and ourselves.

But if God is the absolute wholeness of all that is, then our finite human loves are critical for our experience of God. So while Augustine blames

6. Kimmerer, *Braiding Sweetgrass*, 9.

7. Kimmerer, *Braiding Sweetgrass*, 20.

8. Francis, *Laudato Si'*, §9.

9. Augustine, *City of God*, XIV.11.

10. See Augustine, *Confessions*, VI.15 and VIII.12.

lust for his inability to commit himself fully to God, I rather think human beings simply cannot be fully oriented toward wholeness because of the complexity of human love, which reaches for the physical—the local—even as it participates in the infinite expanse of the whole.

Augustine helpfully underscores that Adam was torn away from the God who is love because human beings discover, express, and experience love within the finite limits of our own bodies. We cannot do otherwise. To make the choice to accompany Eve in sin was a turn away from the whole, yes, but it was also an embodiment of the love that moves all toward wholeness. The whole is contained in and constituted by local relationships: our hearts know this in the restlessness that comes as we negotiate our compromises. Wrestling with these questions is what it means to be human—it is what it means to be like the whole, but not whole.

If we are the earth, conscious of itself, we cannot attend to the whole apart from our material lives. Our consciousness is material, even if it transcends matter, and we are always wrapped up in bodies that are limited. When our eyes were opened to good and evil, the messiness of human existence came into view. With increased consciousness comes the ability to see the harms even our most charitable intentions bring about. I think we all sense this on some level—making our choices and reckoning with their implications is part of our human condition. We know that goodness inheres in evolutive interconnection, but we hesitate to embrace it for fear of its messy vulnerability. That we are concerned at all is indicative of evolving consciousness.

To be human is to grapple with the uncertainties of life. It is when we think we no longer need to grapple with them that we sin. When we lose sight of the whole and absolutize our limitations instead, we destroy the creative possibilities of life.

Acknowledging Our Limits

Adam and Eve, realizing the precarity of their limited selves and unable to relinquish their sense of the whole, make excuses for their actions: "Then God asked: Who told you that you were naked? Have you eaten from the tree of which I had forbidden you to eat? The man replied, 'The woman whom you put here with me—she gave me fruit from the tree, so I ate it.' . . . God then asked the woman: What is this you have done? The woman answered, 'The snake tricked me, so I ate it.'" Augustine tells us that this pride, this failure to acknowledge their choice, is worse than the initial sin itself.[11]

11. Augustine, *City of God*, XIV.14.

Kimmerer offers a helpful reflection on the practical difficulties that attend human consciousness, and emphasizes the importance of copping to our compromises. As she contemplates her efforts to clear out a pond and make it a suitable swimming hole for her daughters, she writes,

> I could work so much faster if I didn't have to stop and pick tadpoles from the tangle of every moral dilemma. I told myself that my intention was not to hurt them; I was just trying to improve the habitat and they were the collateral damage. But my good intentions meant nothing to the tadpoles if they struggled and died in a compost pile. I sighed, but I knew what I had to do. I was driven to this chore by a mothering urge, to make a swimmable pond. In the process, I could hardly sacrifice another mother's children, who, after all, already have a pond to swim in. Now I was not only a pond raker, but also a tadpole plucker. . . . [Upon looking at the muck I was raking under a microscope and discovering tiny creatures impossible to pick out], I bargained with myself over the chain of responsibility and tried to convince myself that their demise served a greater good. . . . As I raked and plucked, it challenged my conviction that all lives are valuable, protozoan or not. As a theoretical matter, I hold this to be true, but on a practical level it gets murky, the spiritual and the pragmatic bumping heads. With every rake I knew that I was prioritizing. Short, single-cell lives were ended because I wanted a clear pond. I'm bigger, I have a rake, so I win. That's not a worldview I readily endorse. But it didn't keep me awake at night, or halt my efforts; I simply acknowledged the choices I was making.[12]

We make these choices daily; it is part of being human. But our sin lies in thinking we do not have to wrestle with them, that this is the way it should be.

Can I take my kids to the store and let them pick out a plastic-wrapped popsicle when I know that pollution is currently ruining our planet? Their syrupy smiles melt my heart, and so I do, sometimes. But I have to acknowledge the choice.

When we fail to acknowledge the harmful effects of our actions, we endorse a hierarchical worldview and become self-righteous and dominative. We make excuses; we argue about why the good we are pursuing is more important than others. If we can stop justifying our position with hierarchical reasoning, we can simply acknowledge and lament those choices as we look for ways to be better. Does this taint the joy of the moment? Maybe. But

---

12. Kimmerer, *Braiding Sweetgrass*, 90.

it also continues the evolution of our consciousness as we try to reconcile the wholeness of being within our limited selves.

Augustine tells us—perhaps in an effort to reassure himself—that "if the will had remained steadfast in the love of that higher and changeless good by which it was illumined to intelligence and kindled into love, it would not have turned away to find satisfaction in itself, and so become frigid and benighted; the woman would not have believed the serpent spoke the truth, nor would the man have preferred the request of his wife to the command of God."[13] In other words, Augustine thinks that if only Adam and Eve had enjoyed their fellowship in God and not departed from God's constancy, they could have avoided the messiness that came about from their human desires and vulnerability. But this is not how life in an evolutive universe works.

Kimmerer's insights are helpful: "We too are always falling. . . . Whether we jump or are pushed, or the edge of the known world just crumbles at our feet, we fall, spinning into someplace new and unexpected. Despite our fears of falling, the gifts of the known world stand by to catch us."[14] This fear of falling, I think, is the root of our tendency to dominate; it is the reason we continue to look at the world through harmful lenses of hierarchy and patriarchy. We do not know that the world will stand by to catch us because we have separated ourselves from the world and convinced ourselves that security comes from clinging tightly to the static pinnacle of being.

Certainly, we use the term hierarchy to describe the organizational structure of many systems that are arranged with a direct link of information and authority; and this is in fact a widespread natural phenomenon.[15] Hierarchy is often useful for nonhuman groups because it can be a mutually beneficial organizational structure. But the hierarchies of the natural world are not static—nature (inclusive of humans, despite our resistance) continues to evolve and expand, enfolding current hierarchies into new ones through new relationships and deeper levels of consciousness. While hierarchical language might help us to conceptualize natural organizing principles, the way the concept has developed in human consciousness is to suggest that organisms at the upper levels of a hierarchy are *superior to* those at the bottom. In the nonhuman world, there is no such valuation.

Hierarchical systems do not suggest that one is inherently better than one's counterparts—there is a cyclical interconnection that undergirds all relationships. The systems are integrated—the "top" layers feed back into

13. Augustine, *City of God*, XIV.13.

14. Kimmerer, *Braiding Sweetgrass*, 9.

15. Zafeiris and Vicsek, "Introduction," in *Why We Live in Hierarchies?*, 1.

those underneath in mutual exchange, and each organism in the chain is critical to and enfolded in the others. None is superior. Although organisms with more layers of consciousness or special capacities may be equipped to direct the activity of their group, the sin of pride cannot corrupt authority in nonhuman beings.

In human hierarchies, however, the system works quite differently. The human lust for domination—the source of pride, the original sin—blinds us to our interconnection and calcifies our hierarchies when we should be open to rethinking them. As Pope Francis writes, "The way natural ecosystems work is exemplary: plants synthesize nutrients which feed herbivores; these in turn become food for carnivores, which produce significant quantities of organic waste which give rise to new generations of plants."[16] This harmonious cycle is broken by the sin of human beings and our disproportionate expansion of domination—by our lust for power and our pursuit of infinite "progress" in our striving to have more rather than to be more.[17] This is precisely why, according to the *Catechism*, our ancestors lost "the grace of original holiness: . . . The harmony in which they had found themselves, thanks to original justice, is now destroyed."[18] Indeed, "the unity of the human race was shattered by sin."[19]

Notice that original justice, that eternal law of which Augustine speaks, is identified as harmony, as unity. Indeed, Augustine identifies God as the "common good of all": "You rid us of our evil habits and forgive our sins when we confess to you. You listen to the groans of the prisoners and free us from the chains which we have forged for ourselves. This you do for us unless we toss our heads against you in the illusion of liberty and in our greed for gain, at the risk of losing all, love our own good better than you yourself, who are the common good of all."[20] To live in right relationship, then, requires us to acknowledge our original sin—the pride which accepts or asserts our limited existence as the whole without apology—and embrace instead the evolutive grace of God that draws all of creation toward wholeness.

Of course, we limited creatures will never be wholly successful in this effort. To be human is to reckon with our inability to love unconditionally, to grapple with the uncertainty of the choices we must make when expressing our love. Indeed, Augustine takes these limitations to be consequences of original sin: "My soul," he exclaims, "why do you face about and follow

16. Francis, *Laudato Si'*, §22.

17. See Paul VI, *Populorum progressio*.

18. CCC §399–400.

19. CCC §56.

20. Augustine, *Confessions*, III.8.

the lead of the flesh? Turn forward, and let it follow you! Whatever you feel through the senses of the flesh you only feel in part. It delights you, but it is only a part and you have no knowledge of the whole. To punish you this just limit has been fixed for the senses of your body."[21] That we can acknowledge our limits and strive to foster wholeness is due only to the grace of the Incarnate Christ, who unites the whole within the limited capacity of humanity.

CHRIST: THE EMBODIED WHOLE

Although he had no concept of evolutionary science, Augustine's account of creation is surprisingly compatible with contemporary knowledge. Augustine infers from the Genesis creation account that "the unformed state through which things temporarily pass as they change from form to form is not unplanned. . . . The wasting and growth by which creatures succeed one another in the course of time is something that contributes to the beauty of the world."[22] He goes on, "The unformed creation had been set apart precisely so that still other beings might be formed from it."[23] And, again, he emphasizes, "The beauty of the ages is unfolded by the coming and passing of things."[24] Though we struggle to contain the changes wrought by time, Augustine assures us that "were your carnal perception able to grasp the whole, were it not . . . confined to its due part of the whole, you would long for whatever exists only in the present to pass away, so that you might find greater joy in the totality."[25]

Of the creation of human beings, Augustine writes, "When the eternal and unchangeable wisdom . . . enters into spiritual and rational creatures . . . so that with [wisdom's] light they may shine, then in the reason which has been illuminated there is a new state introduced."[26] In other words, creation evolves into ever new forms, and human beings constitute a "new state"—a new kind of being—because we are imbued with wisdom. Human beings are thus "linked together by a common fellowship based on a common nature" that is grounded in their capacity for virtue infused by wisdom, as well as their weakness.[27] Wisdom here, we should note, is Christ. As Augustine writes elsewhere, "Wisdom condescended to adapt [itself] to our weakness,

21. Augustine, *Confessions*, IV.11.
22. Augustine, "On the Literal Interpretation," 1.17.34, in Augustine, *On Genesis*.
23. Augustine, "On the Literal Interpretation," 1.17.35, in Augustine, *On Genesis*.
24. Augustine, "On the Literal Interpretation," 1.8.14, in Augustine, *On Genesis*.
25. Augustine, *Confessions*, IV.11.
26. Augustine, "On the Literal Interpretation," 1.17.32, in Augustine, *On Genesis*.
27. Augustine, *City of God*, XVIII.2.

and to show us a pattern of holy life in the form of our own humanity."[28] Our very humanity, then, is tied to Christ's humility, embedded in the dust of the earth from which we are formed.

Putting all of this together, Augustine's account affirms the adaptation of creatures and the development of new forms. It includes human beings as part of this evolving creation, with the distinctive qualities of rationality and free will. It recognizes that our essential humanness comes not from dominating the world, but from embracing our interconnection with all of creation in Christ.

By denying the new state of humanity—the "true self" made in the image of God—and adopting structures of dominance rather than interconnection, human beings failed to stanch "the flow of habit, by which [we are] wasting away to death."[29] Indeed, our tendency to dominate is evolutionary residue that results in our failure to use the gift of consciousness to evolve toward wholeness, through vulnerable love. But by putting on Christ, we open ourselves to the grace of conversion that calls us beyond our habits and social customs and calls into question the order of hierarchy and the dominative tendencies thereof.

Given what scientists are discovering about matter and energy, the same elements present in the big bang are enfolded in our flesh, so on a visceral level, we are linked to Jesus's body through elements that can be traced back to the creation of the world. Christ's "incarnation witnesses to a divine destiny seeded in our very flesh," as M. Shawn Copeland reflects, and this "makes the infinite God present, disrupts every pleasure of hierarchy, economy, cultural domination, racial violence, gender oppression, and abuse of sexual others."[30] Cosmological consciousness can help us to direct our love toward ever-inclusive wholeness, corresponding to the expansive, evolutive, incarnational creativity of God, who is love.

The wisdom of Christ reveals the intrinsic worth of all of creation and enables human beings to image God in our relationships through embodying interdependency with creative and life-sustaining activity. When we choose instead to affirm as whole our limited sense of the good, domination becomes a willful act and therefore a sinful one. As Russell puts it, sin lies in the inability of human beings to accept our limits and embrace our interdependency: "Our original sin," she writes, "is that rather than enfolded wholeness and love, we have enfolded an implicit sense of division,

---

28. Augustine, *On Christian Doctrine*, 1.11.

29. Augustine, *Confessions*, VIII.7.

30. Copeland, *Enfleshing Freedom*, 65.

fragmentation, and prejudice against the other."[31] In other words, those convictions or desires to which we cling prevent us from opening ourselves to evolutive grace and the humility upon which our humanity depends.

In Augustine's account, we find the seeds of cosmic consciousness, despite what we might call his own limited vision. Augustine notes, "Your beauty drew me to you, but soon I was dragged away from you by my own weight. . . . The weight I carried was the habit of the flesh. But your memory remained with me and I had no doubt at all that you were the one to whom I should cling, only I was not yet able to cling to you."[32] The memory of the whole is enfolded in each of us, but the habits of the flesh that limit our moral vision to what we ourselves can grasp blind us to its beauty. As Erika Kidd recognizes, Augustine warns that our carnal perception "tempts us to think that the passing [of all things] is absolute, drawing everything into permanent loss."[33]

And so, when Augustine declares that "we bear the remnants of our darkness in our bodies, which are dead things in virtue of our guilt,"[34] perhaps we can understand him to gesture toward the need for an expansive horizon of consciousness—one that is not constrained by the spatial and temporal limits of our physical, individual bodies, nor the experiential limits of our minds. Perhaps the darkness is of our own making as we shut our eyes against the light of the whole, stopping ourselves from confessing our shortcomings or responding with hope to emerging consciousness.

This may be why in Augustine's thought, as Hampson and Hoff explain, "there is a dynamic at work in which 'scientia' (the knowledge and love of created things) eventually gives way to 'sapientia' (wisdom, the love of sacred and divine things)."[35] Loving with an eye toward the whole means that we never can limit ourselves to a purely materialistic idolatry: we cannot love the parts without reference to the whole; and yet, the whole is enfolded in each part, and each part reveals something about it. If, as Augustine tells us, "we catch sight of the truth as [it] is known through . . . creation,"[36] surely we learn that the order of truth is one of evolutive, interconnected relationality.

31. Russell, *Source of All Love*, 24.

32. Augustine, *Confessions*, VII.17.

33. Kidd, "Book IV: Fugitive Beauty," in Meconi, *Augustine's Confessions*, 85.

34. Augustine, *Confessions*, XIII.14.

35. Hampson and Hoff, "Whose Self?," 559. See Augustine, *On the Trinity*, XII.4.25.

36. Augustine, *Confessions*, VII.10.

In her poem, "Remember,"[37] the poet Joy Harjo offers a litany intended to help us call to mind our interconnectedness. Her invocation to memory is not simply a mental exercise; it requires embodied response. To remember, she exhorts us to engage our physical being—birthing, breathing, struggling, talking, listening, dancing. In other words, memory and hope are incarnate. Teresa Maya, CCVI, expresses this beautifully: "To understand the future we need to take time to remember. 'Remember' in Spanish comes from re-cordis, to run through the heart once more.... Memory is the sacrament of presence."[38] Deep memory that reflects our authentic human nature in relationship to all life in the cosmos requires our active engagement and participation in the recognition that we come from the earth and that our presence, too, will be carried into the future. In this deep memory, Maya reflects, "we will find the seeds of hope we need to sow" in the present, to create the future.[39]

Christ, in the incarnation, passion, and resurrection, reveals the whole to us, drawing us toward oneness and reconciling our memory, hope, and present response. For Augustine, as Michael Scanlon explains, Christ's incarnation means that "memory becomes anticipation, and the longing of the will for beatitude reaches out in hope for the future fulfillment."[40] Christ—the wisdom of the cosmos, the spirit of love made flesh—unites the wholeness of being within the consciousness of humanity. "The cosmic Christ," Laurie Brink, OP, suggests, "is the fulfilled potentiality seeded in the creation, germinated in the human Jesus, and blossomed in evolutionary consciousness.... The cosmic Christ is the ultimate both/and. Described in Scripture, born out in tradition, and verified in our personal experiences of prayer and encounter. But the cosmic Christ is also the direction forward."[41] Christ breaks the chains of divisive habits and reconciles us to the grace of original harmony, offering us the way and the goal of human love through embodying in Jesus all that is, was, and will be.

Reflecting on her community's Christmas Eve ritual in 2014, in the midst of brutal and tragic war and terrorism in the Middle East, Flaherty makes this point tangible:

> As the 2014 Christmas Eve liturgy at the Blauvelt Dominican Motherhouse in New York was about to begin, a small burlap

37. Harjo, "Remember," in Harjo, She Had Some Horses, 35.

38. Maya, "Vision," 4.

39. Maya, "Vision," 4.

40. Scanlon, "Arendt's Augustine," in Caputo and Scanlon, Augustine and Postmodernism, 161.

41. Brink, Heavens Are Telling, 156.

bag filled with the soil of Iraq was placed in the congregation's
crèche. This symbolic action was not only a prayer for the suffering Iraqi people, but also a reminder that in the midst of the
terrorizing violence, divisions, and displacements that besiege
this ancient homeland of Christianity, God becomes flesh and
dwells within Iraq today.[42]

In the soil, in the humble crèche, in the Iraqi people, in the gathering of
sisters with hearts unfolded, in the suffering of violence, in the love that
draws all toward wholeness and healing—Christ is present.

In our community of faith, Christ's real presence in the Eucharist
makes clear to us that there is an absolute wholeness of being, which our finite imaginations cannot comprehend and our limited bodies cannot grasp.
Augustine calls this the whole Christ—*totus Christus*—which, as Allan
Fitzgerald, OSA, observes, "emphasized the unity of Christ and the Church,"
embracing "the time of Christ on earth and in heaven and [including] those
who prefigured, foretold and awaited for his coming."[43] New cosmology
takes us even further.

As the whole incarnates a piece of bread, we recognize that the material world *matters*; that it is infused always and everywhere with Christ.
When we revere Christ in the Eucharist, we revere the body that holds elements present at the big bang, DNA from nonhuman ancestors, and the
consciousness of the world, whole and unbroken. We acknowledge that we
are the ones who carry them into the future, linking the past and future in
the fullness of the present moment through the love of Christ that draws us.
We recognize that we belong to the Body of Christ, and we know that we
are not Christ. We kneel in reverence, joining in adoration with the communion of saints, whose lives are enfolded into our own as we are carried
together in Christ, the whole. To see God, then, is to immerse ourselves
in this world. Johnson offers this profound insight: "Biologically speaking,
new life continuously comes from death, over time. Theologically speaking,
the cross gives grounds to hope that the presence of the living God in the
midst of pain bears creation forward with unimaginable promise."[44]

Kay O'Connell, SSND, in a poem inspired by Seamus Heaney's "Dig-
ging," passionately describes the unfolding of the universe in love as *Christ
Omega, the ultimate point of this evolving universe / the Fire that drives*

---

42. Flaherty et al., "We Have Family in Iraq."

43. Fitzgerald, "Priesthood in Saint Augustine," in Ouellet, *For a Fundamental Theology*, 5.

44. Johnson, *Ask the Beasts*, 210.

cosmogenesis on to its Pleroma / its unimaginable fulfillment in God.[45] In Christ, we can remember. In Christ, we can hope. In Christ, we are called to respond through our particular bodies to the evolving wholeness that is our future.

PAUSE FOR REFLECTION

Take a moment to reflect on what you read.

- What is drawing your attention? What words, phrases, or concepts stand out to you? Are any new insights stirring in you?

- How do memory, hope, and present response come together in Christ? In the earth? In you? Does cosmological imagination help to enrich your response?

- Are there other ways in which you can imagine cosmological consciousness enriching your interpretation of tradition?

45. O'Connell, "Reflections on Integral Ecology."

5

Choosing Unity with LCWR

A Practical Conversion

Prophecy and hope dance in the endless cycle compassion weaves
into the future promised by God.

—Teresa Maya, CCVI

It is one thing to theologize about a paradigm of interconnection; it is
quite another to practice it. Indeed, this paradigm might even seem idealis-
tic to some—Carey, for example, calls it "feel-good, diffuse spirituality."[1] But
to relinquish power and certitude and continuously embrace the vulnerability of relational integrity, one must be rooted in a very practical and
embodied commitment to follow Christ. As we remember our evolutive
roots and emergent potential in Christ, we can approach relationships from
a position of interconnection rather than hierarchy, responding to others
in love and vulnerability, rather than self-righteousness and hostility—and
this often feels anything but good, resonating more with the suffering of
Christ's passion than the hope of resurrection.

I confess that self-righteousness has always been a vice of mine. I
don't like to be wrong, and I tend to become annoyed when others don't see

1. Carey, "Women Religious."

things my way and angry when I am accused of erring. Partly, this is because I dread being the cause of someone else's troubles; mainly, it is because fallibility implies vulnerability, and I like to be in control.

Recently, for example, my husband and I got into an argument. Why? Because he told me I had offended him. My initial response was to become defensive: *that's not what I intended to do, and you shouldn't be offended for reasons x, y, and z.* Though I tried to be sensitive and compassionate, refraining from biting language or aggressive tone, I felt anger start to rise because I felt misunderstood. And I suppose that is the heart of the matter: *I* felt misunderstood, so I was angry. I was turned inward, focused on keeping my record clean. If instead I reached out toward my husband, perhaps I could meet him in a space of deeper understanding. It does not matter that I didn't mean to hurt him—I did hurt him. And if I can listen and learn rather than shut him out in anger, our understanding of one another will grow in love.

Love casts out fear—and isn't anger most often a response to fear? In my case, fears of rejection and imperfection are at its root. It is anything but righteous. If I respond this way to my husband, my relationship with whom is premised on a vow to image God by entering continuously into deeper relationship that exudes in ever-expansive love, what hope is there for my response to neighbors known only through news reports, or those "enemies" I cannot trust to approach me with reciprocal care?

As I served with the SSND, the United States was tearing itself in two—this had been an ongoing endeavor, of course, but the tensions were reaching a boiling point toward the end of the 2010s. I began my work for the order during the second year of Donald Trump's presidency, around the time the Intergovernmental Panel on Climate Change issued its 2018 Special Report, which warned that we have approximately one decade to reverse our current climate trajectory or life on earth will be irrevocably altered—and, indeed, it already has been for many people as well as nonhuman species.[2] Other key events during my tenure with the SSND included the traumatic government-ordered separations of migrant children from their parents; the COVID-19 pandemic; the brutal murder of George Floyd at the hands of police officer Derek Chauvin, which set off a nationwide racial reckoning; multiple high-profile mass shootings (and hundreds of underreported ones); the election of Joe Biden to the presidency; and the armed invasion of the US Capitol on January 6, 2021.

Each of these events generated widespread action or resistance, but deeply entrenched partisanship informed the way in which people

2. Intergovernmental Panel on Climate Change, "Special Report."

responded to them. As people asserted their own version of events and claimed their response as the only option, our capacity for dialogue diminished and we came to inhabit what appeared to be separate versions of reality. If my neighbor rejects the factual reality of our shared life, it is difficult to see how we can engage in dialogue, which always involves at least the existence of shared definitions.

Unfortunately, the hostility and division that bifurcated the country rent the church as well. Catholics are now split nearly equally along party lines, and our positions on issues are informed more by partisan talking points than our faith. We became willing to sacrifice our sacramental unity for the sake of political power.[3]

It is easy to be angry. How can *they* not see what I see? How can the other be so arrogant, so hateful? I find it difficult to imagine what unity could even look like in such times.

I confess that widespread Christian support for policies and actions that directly and traumatically harmed others—separating migrant children, gutting measures to combat climate change, refusing to wear a mask or receive a vaccine during a pandemic—had me questioning my affiliation with the church. And I was sickened as I watched self-proclaimed Christians violently storming the Capitol building to disrupt a democratic process, invoking the name of Jesus to bless their violence. No amount of theologizing about the unity of the "Body of Christ" could reconcile the Jesus I know with theirs. I had come to understand that if we are not concerned primarily with countering actual injustice toward those who are made poor and vulnerable, if we are concerned more with maintaining our own power, then we are not following Christ.

However, much of my work for peace and justice at this time focused on the need to approach these issues with charity: in light of my Augustinian training, I maintained that rightly ordered love leads to right relationships, and this requires us to maintain an emotional posture capable of sustaining relations with others, even those whom we count as enemies. Indeed, Augustine denounces the Donatists of his time, who "hate peace" because they "tear our unity apart."[4] Their motives for seceding from the church, he recognizes, include "the desire to be righteous, and not be mixed up with the unrighteous," but this is in direct contradiction to the Catholic voice, which calls for unity and the humility that fosters it.[5] But still, as these Christians in our era assert their dominance and profess falsehoods in the

---

3. This analysis was developed previously in Bonnette, "Now Is the Time."

4. Augustine, *Essential Expositions*, 119.9.

5. See Augustine, *Essential Expositions*, 119.9.

name of God, righteous anger threatens to consume me. And, clearly, the sentiment cuts both ways.

During the turmoil of the past few years, even Augustine's ethic of rightly ordered love and right relationships, as I understood it, seemed to reinforce my *libido dominandi* as I clung vehemently to my own sense of "right." Is it possible, or even desirable, to engage in dialogue with those I know to be fundamentally *wrong*, particularly when their error results in direct harm to others? Do I even want to be "woven together" with *them*? As the group Solidarity with Sisters recognizes, "the choice of nonviolence is most difficult when we thoughtfully believe that people who have a lot of power are misusing it in ways that harm those who are poor and vulnerable. Can we stay nonjudgmental and nonconfrontational then? Can we find ways to speak truth in love as we work for change? The effort tests our commitment and creativity."[6]

I confess that I failed this test more than once. At times, my anger over actions morphed into disrespect of persons—I don't always know how to maintain that distinction, and I have hurt people because of it. In my zeal for justice, I sometimes have failed to stay charitable toward opponents, or to be fully present and open to those in my intimate circle. Though my sense of justice is partial, I can be quick to maintain its completeness. And in my efforts to be the hands and feet of Christ, I have neglected at times to reflect Christ's heart—a heart that is always open to encounter.[7]

I know I am not the only one who has lost friends to the cultural chasm bifurcating our church and our nation. I mourn relationships with those dear ones, with whom it seems impossible to find common ground—or at least, the effort it would take to do so seems too immense to even try. It is certainly possible that by committing to what I call "the highest good" and ordering my loves accordingly, I miss opportunities to build authentic relationships.

When our moral values are ordered by truth, it can appear that engagement across these battle lines is impossible or unnecessary. In other words, when our relationships are ordered within a hierarchical framework, we cannot help but assert our perspective as true when we feel we have knowledge of the One. But when our relationships are ordered toward further relationship in the wholeness of being, our own sense of right becomes less important than encountering the other.

Embracing cosmic consciousness allows for creativity—for our limits and vulnerabilities to inspire new relationships and ways of being in the

6. Hughes, "Spiritual Journey," in Sanders, *However Long the Night,* 149.

7. This paragraph is adapted from Bonnette, "Where Do We Go from Here?"

world. Perhaps the most effective way to underscore the importance of adopting a paradigm of interconnection is to observe its effects on the actions of those who embody it. In the integrity, humility, and creativity of women religious, for example, we see this cosmological spirituality exemplified and the distinction between interconnection and hierarchy is put into stark relief.

The response of the Leadership Conference of Women Religious (LCWR) during the Vatican investigation of their activity from 2009 to 2015 offers a particularly compelling example of choosing love and humility over power. In the face of humiliation and derision, they maintained a posture of reconciliation, rather than self-righteousness. Claiming the metaphor of the Weaving God, the leadership of LCWR recognize now that "the prevailing ecclesial environment [at the time] was one in which expression of valid differences often carried judgment concerning loyalty, orthodoxy, legitimacy. The moment suggested an urgent need to weave the contrasting colors of that tension into a tapestry with some coherent pattern."[8] Reflecting on their ordeal and the theological framework that guided them through it provides a helpful way to imagine what it might mean to embody integrity and act on conviction, even as we remain humble and open to change and encounter.

In the activities of these women religious, we see an expression of love ordered toward wholeness.

LOVE'S INTEGRITY

In 2009, the Congregation for the Doctrine of the Faith (CDF), the office charged with protecting the patrimony of the Catholic Church, notified the Leadership Conference of Women Religious (LCWR), whose member congregations represent nearly 80 percent of women religious in the United States, that it would be conducting an investigation into their activity. This initial investigation, which they emphasized was motivated by "a sincere concern for the life of faith" of these congregations, concluded in 2012 when the CDF identified the following issues of concern:

First, the CDF objected to keynote speakers at LCWR events who, they claimed, sometimes offered problematic statements and "serious theological, even doctrinal errors," which challenged "core Catholic beliefs."[9] The primary worry focused on proponents of new cosmology. In the openness

---

8. Farrell, "Tapestry of Contrasting Colors," in Sanders, *However Long the Night*, 86.

9. CDF, "Doctrinal Assessment."

of women religious to this emerging spirituality, the CDF exhorted their brethren, "Pastors of the Church should also see . . . a cry for help."[10]

Second, the CDF noted "the absence of initiatives by the LCWR aimed at promoting the reception of the Church's teaching, especially on difficult issues such as Pope John Paul II's Apostolic Letter *Ordinatio sacerdotalis* [which closed the question of women's ordination] and Church teaching about homosexuality."[11] The CDF found fault with the LCWR for prioritizing social issues other than those on which the bishops were focused—specifically, they found that "while there has been a great deal of work on the part of LCWR promoting issues of social justice in harmony with the Church's social doctrine," their advocacy work did not focus enough on countering abortion, homosexuality, or calls to instate women to the priesthood.[12]

Then-president of LCWR, Sister Pat Farrell, OSF, called this criticism "unfair," and noted that women religious give their lives in service of promoting human dignity, including that of the unborn, though they may question policies that are more pro-fetus than pro-life and though they raise some concerns about the church's teaching on gender and sexuality.[13] But the CDF emphasized that "the bishops, who are the Church's authentic teachers of faith and morals" are not to be publicly challenged or questioned, and the prophetic witness of women religious is meant to be directed only outward toward the public, not inward toward the institutional church.[14]

Finally, the CDF censured the LCWR for their "radical feminism" that risks "distorting faith in Jesus and his loving Father who sent his Son for the salvation of the world"—one can hardly miss the extreme emphasis on masculinity, here. The CDF also rebuked feminist "commentaries on patriarchy" that "distort the way in which Jesus has structured the sacramental life in the Church."[15] To prove the point, the CDF required the work of the LCWR to be overseen by one of their delegates until 2015.

The LCWR, for its part, reported being "stunned that our belief in [Catholic] doctrine was being called into question. We did not recognize ourselves in CDF's description as stated in the mandate."[16] Affirming their deep commitment to the church's rich deposit of faith, the LCWR lamented that "the men with whom we were speaking interpreted the way we prayed

10. CDF, "Doctrinal Assessment."

11. CDF, "Doctrinal Assessment."

12. CDF, "Doctrinal Assessment."

13. Gross, "American Nun Responds."

14. CDF, "Doctrinal Assessment."

15. CDF, "Doctrinal Assessment."

16. Mock, "Common Journey," in Sanders, *However Long the Night*, 57.

together and spoke about God and the things of God as a violation of Catholic orthodoxy."[17] In fact, the LCWR had been "encouraging member congregations to study and pray with the documents of Vatican II," which they recognized as resulting "in well-developed spiritualities consistent with each congregation's charism."[18] And they saw this as a gift: for women religious, "theology and spirituality are vital disciplines informing and influencing how we live our lives according to the Gospel."[19]

The call to share their spiritual insights with the church and the world is one of the unique vocations of religious congregations. Farrell sums up the experience poignantly: "As women religious, our love for the church, though questioned by some, was deep and undeniable for us. The mystical, prophetic charism of religious life emerged within the church, a gift in service to the church and the world. To feel apart from or at odds with the institutional church was painful and unacceptable."[20] And so, the LCWR had to grapple with the question that forms the backdrop for our current political and ecclesial climate: "How does one go about developing an authentic relationship with a group of people who, in our experience, took words out of context and acted against us on that misrepresentation of truth?"[21]

The National Catholic Reporter printed at the time that "at the conflict's heart is a difference in approach to hierarchical chain of command: the top-down, morals-emphasizing Vatican versus the collegial, social-justice oriented nuns."[22] And Mary Gordon put it bluntly: "The Catholic hierarchy [imagined] their censure of the nuns would be accepted obediently."[23] Indeed, she goes on, "Powerful women who seem to be taking over traditionally masculine roles, asserting that they don't need to be subservient to men as in the past, are one more threat to the Catholic patriarchy. What better way to re-establish masculine authority than to demonstrate the ability to dominate women?"[24]

When writing the initial draft of this chapter, I, too, focused on the oppressive use of patriarchal power that is so clearly antithetical to the Gospel. Resentment fueled my writing as my fingers drilled down on keys, crafting sentences that dripped with condescension.

17. Mock, "Common Journey," in Sanders, *However Long the Night*, 57.
18. Mock, "Common Journey," in Sanders, *However Long the Night*, 57.
19. Mock, "Common Journey," in Sanders, *However Long the Night*, 58.
20. Farrell, "Tapestry of Contrasting Colors," in Sanders, *However Long the Night*, 86.
21. Mock, "Common Journey," in Sanders, *However Long the Night*, 57.
22. Hall, "Sister Elizabeth Johnson."
23. Gordon, "Francis and the Nuns."
24. Gordon, "Francis and the Nuns."

But these assessments fail to capture the grace of the moment. Certainly, the hierarchical model of church relations lends itself to this power struggle. It is easy to accuse the bishops of seeking to "re-establish masculine authority"; on the other hand, some might find it easy to side with the bishops: if the nuns are in fact ignoring the Magisterium, they should be censured. Either way, we fall into the trap of division. We frame the event as a power struggle, pick a side, and hope that "our side" wins—for the good of the church.

The LCWR, however, did not respond with cynicism and resentment; instead, they asked, "To what [is] God inviting us at this moment in time?"[25] Marcia Allen, CSJ, and Florence Deacon, OSF, recall that "the temptation to justify ourselves publicly was always present. So many of the charges were egregious misrepresentations of facts; however, a lifetime of discernment and living out the spiritual life had taught us that self-knowledge reveals the redeeming need for compassion and forgiveness—beginning with oneself."[26] And so, rather than assert themselves in self-righteousness, which is simply another manifestation of the *libido dominandi*, the women of LCWR remained open to the grace of the Spirit. "As events unfolded," they recall, "we were convinced that love for church and Gospel must lead us in our responses."[27]

It was easy to be angry. But Farrell recalls that at the National Assembly in 2012, after the CDF mandate was imposed, LCWR came to recognize "the grace of not seeing a way out of the challenge we faced."[28] As Allen and Deacon describe it,

> When the prospect of a dialogue or any kind of understanding seemed most impossible and the temptation was to retaliate in self-aggrandizing arguments of righteousness, the conference members in assembly chose a counterintuitive measure. The assembly participants invoked the Holy Spirit and prayed: "We abandon ourselves into your hands, O God. Keep our hearts soft and our minds open, as we wait for the truth of this moment to reveal itself." Praying for soft hearts in tough times seems a doubtful strategy but it does denote the disposition of the conference to be open to the action of God in their midst—and in the midst of the trouble they were experiencing. This predisposition to grace was the underpinning of the faith journey through

25. Farrell, "Gift and Challenge," in Sanders, *However Long the Night*, 48.

26. Allen and Deacon, "Relationships Matter," in Sanders, *However Long the Night*, 74.

27. Allen and Deacon, "Relationships Matter," in Sanders, *However Long the Night*, 70.

28. Farrell, "Gift and Challenge," in Sanders, *However Long the Night*, 50.

the years, and it manifested in a stance of compassion rather than violence that the event would seem naturally to evoke.[29]

The members of LCWR chose—continuously, and with not a little effort—to frame this experience in terms of relationship, not power. In response to an unexpected affront, these women chose unity over division. Why? Because their working theological paradigm is one of interconnection, rather than hierarchy. A paradigm of hierarchy lends itself to the violence of power struggles; a paradigm of interconnection requires humility.

The LCWR and its member congregations have been cultivating this relational identity for decades, engaging in "corporate study and prayer rooted in sound theology [which] became the springboard for articulating evolving images of God."[30] These images "bore fruit in an incarnational spirituality which focuses on the Spirit alive within all of humankind and reflected in creation, and especially in the faces of those who are made poor by injustice."[31] This consciousness has resulted in ministry directed toward unity, and also in the development of participative structures and communal discernment processes.

Women religious have imagined and articulated an evolving way of understanding God—and by extension who we are in relation to one another and our world—and the emergent paradigm allows for authentic humility and integrity. The changes to their organizational order, Farrell notes, "while neither foolproof nor without error, offered some corrective to the authoritarianism which lent itself to domination and the abuse of power."[32] Farrell reflects that these practices "have helped our congregations move through times of massive change together. It has not been easy. We are still learning. But the process has been enriching and most of us can no longer imagine functioning within more hierarchical frameworks of decision-making."[33] Meanwhile, she observes, "The institutional church has not undergone the same re-visioning of structures of authority and obedience."[34] In a time of massive cultural and ecclesial upheaval, imagining new ways of relating is critical for maintaining integrity. As Brink recognizes, "If we accept that we live in an unfinished universe, in the midst of evolution, where at the

29. Allen and Deacon, "Relationships Matter," in Sanders, However Long the Night, 78.

30. Mock, "Common Journey," in Sanders, However Long the Night, 57.

31. Mock, "Common Journey," in Sanders, However Long the Night, 58.

32. Farrell, "Gift and Challenge," in Sanders, However Long the Night, 47.

33. Farrell, "Tapestry of Contrasting Colors," in Sanders, However Long the Night, 91.

34. Farrell, "Tapestry of Contrasting Colors," in Sanders, However Long the Night, 91.

very heart of matter is probability not certainty, then our very structures, processes, and programs must reflect our emerging reality."[35]

In responding to the CDF mandate, LCWR's commitment to communal discernment was instrumental to their response. Rather than responding with knee-jerk reactions or by seeking power, the sisters recognized the need "to entrust ourselves to the larger divine movement which was holding and carrying us. It was evident that we were dealing with something larger than ourselves. We were invited to hold the tensions and to discover unseen ways beyond polarization and dualities."[36] By listening for the Spirit emerging through their communal presence and dialogue, they "were able to see together with the eyes of our common heart more than any one of us could have seen alone,"[37] and "were carried together in a direction which only gradually showed itself and which stretched beyond our own effort."[38]

And so, Farrell explains, "What was slowly distilled in the process [of communal discernment] was the group sense to proceed in dialogue with the bishop delegates so long as LCWR's mission and integrity would not be compromised."[39] Recognizing that dialogue is meaningless when we enter with preconceived ideas of what is right, having determined already the best course of action and endeavoring to convince those who disagree to see it our way, the LCWR leadership committed to keeping "soft hearts" open to listening and understanding. At the heart of their relational posture was "a readiness to be transformed, a willingness to be changed by an encounter with another."[40] But what does it mean to maintain integrity while being willing to change? Here, again, we are reminded that our integrity—our wholeness—is tied to our vulnerability.

Referencing theologian Beatrice Bruteau, Allen and Deacon emphasize that to be "a person (from the Latin *per* and *sonare* meaning 'to sound through')" is to embody "fundamental openness. A person is a replication of the Trinitarian *perichoresis* in that persons are not made of building blocks but complicated webs of energy relations. . . . Personhood is fulfilled in relationships and communion."[41] In other words, we embody the fullness of our dignity when we are vulnerable to love and open to change. And for the sisters, this relational vulnerability did not extend only to their members or

35. Brink, *Heavens Are Telling*, 167.
36. Farrell, "Gift and Challenge," in Sanders, *However Long the Night*, 50.
37. Farrell, "Gift and Challenge," in Sanders, *However Long the Night*, 51.
38. Farrell, "Gift and Challenge," in Sanders, *However Long the Night*, 52.
39. Farrell, "Gift and Challenge," in Sanders, *However Long the Night*, 51.
40. Farrell, "Gift and Challenge," in Sanders, *However Long the Night*, 53.
41. Allen and Deacon, "Relationships Matter," in Sanders, *However Long the Night*, 80.

the supportive public. Instead, "The internal dynamic for LCWR's purposes was that relationships matter: relationships with God, self, the Catholic Church, the conference and its mission and members, CDF, the officers of CDF, and the bishop delegates."[42]

Recognizing that "the drive to be in relationship lies at the center of our being,"[43] LCWR approached the crisis with the determination to "set aside our individuality, that egotistical self-protective shield, and begin to exercise true personhood—openness and transparent honesty in relationships with others."[44] Indeed, Allen and Deacon observe that "after lifetimes shaped by theological studies and communal practices, the leadership of LCWR had an intuitive comprehension of the real meaning of person—our own personhood—in that it was through our own openness to potential communion that we were able to continue to approach CDF with the intent and hope for dialogue."[45]

Allen and Deacon note that "humility and openness, curiosity and patience, fidelity to the process and one another, resilience, courage, and generosity of person" marked the LCWR response.[46] This posture, they suggest, reflects what Scilla Elworthy terms "a certain 'feminine intelligence,' available to men as well as women, that enables conflicted parties to experience a shift in consciousness and thus bring about reconciliation and peace."[47] Note that rather than complementing "masculine" gifts, this feminine intelligence invites all people to a more authentic embodiment of personhood. In this sense, I suppose it is "radical"—taking us back to our roots.

By practicing a relational posture and eschewing hierarchical models in their theology and spirituality, as well as their organizational structures, members of LCWR walked in their authentic dignity as persons with integrity, called to wholeness. And it should give us hope that "observers saw these attitudes emerge and unfold, mature, and become effective as the years wore on."[48] There is always room for growth.

At the end of the six-year ordeal, the CDF and LCWR issued a joint final report that reflected the fruits of so much labor. The document concludes, "The commitment of LCWR leadership to its crucial role in service

42. Allen and Deacon, "Relationships Matter," in Sanders, *However Long the Night*, 79.
43. Mock, "Common Journey," in Sanders, *However Long the Night*, 56.
44. Allen and Deacon, "Relationships Matter," Sanders, in *However Long the Night*, 69.
45. Allen and Deacon, "Relationships Matter," in Sanders, *However Long the Night*, 80.
46. Allen and Deacon, "Relationships Matter," in Sanders, *However Long the Night*, 79.
47. Allen and Deacon, "Relationships Matter," in Sanders, *However Long the Night*, 79.
48. Allen and Deacon, "Relationships Matter," in Sanders, *However Long the Night*, 79.

to the mission and membership of the Conference will continue to guide and strengthen LCWR's witness to the great vocation of Religious Life, to its sure foundation in Christ, and to ecclesial communion."[49] And in the CDF's press release about the conclusion of the ordeal, then-prefect Cardinal Müller affirmed that "the Congregation is confident that LCWR has made clear its mission to support its member Institutes by fostering a vision of religious life that is centered on the Person of Jesus Christ and is rooted in the Tradition of the Church. It is this vision that makes religious women and men radical witnesses to the Gospel, and, therefore, is essential for the flourishing of religious life in the Church."[50]

In LCWR's response to CDF, we see the cosmic consciousness of interconnection and evolution at work:

> Relationships mattered. Both leaders and members of the conference understood the implicate order in which we lived: all were connected by an intrinsic bond that made us one whether we would accept it or not. . . . Nor did we forget what Elworthy would call regenerative power, that is, the implications of our actions and words for the larger church or for the world itself. Although we were in the immediate sphere wholly preoccupied with the needs of our relationship with the CDF, we also knew that whatever we did affected the greater world.[51]

Enfolded into their own integrity was the integrity of the church, the CDF, and the world.

By choosing openness and humility over self-righteousness and control, the LCWR's integrity nurtured those relationships and bore witness to the power of vulnerable love. Thus, they could commit to seeing "the doctrinal assessment process through to the end, trusting that loose strands seemingly going nowhere were being woven into some unseen pattern by the divine energy carrying us."[52] As Farrell puts it so beautifully,

> Our God who draws the human family forward toward greater life and wholeness was at work in the process we were living, beyond what we could know. We learned that as we gave ourselves over to what was being asked of us for the greater good,

49. CDF and LCWR, "Joint Final Report."

50. Vatican Press Office, "Press Release on the Final Report." Note that Cardinal Müller has since been accused of covering up or maintaining inadequate oversight over priests accused of sexual assault under his jurisdiction, and Pope Francis declined to renew his position as prefect of the CDF.

51. Allen and Deacon, "Relationships Matter," in Sanders, *However Long the Night*, 79.

52. Farrell, "Tapestry of Contrasting Colors," in Sanders, *However Long the Night*, 88.

we would be given what we needed. And what we needed then, now, and always was a deepening capacity to love: to love all that manifested as messy, broken, or divisive.[53]

In the response of LCWR to the CDF mandate, we see the cosmological imagination at work, insisting on personal integrity that leads to wholeness.

Solidarity with Sisters recognizes "LCWR's capacity to love what is broken while imagining wholeness and healing that don't yet exist."[54] And as Allen and Deacon reflect,

> LCWR's best strategy . . . was a real expression of personhood and an expression of love that is self-gift for the benefit of others. This led to partnerships in a continuing conversation that became open and honest dialogue about real concerns; reverenced the essential person within the individuals with whom we engaged; and fostered truth-seeking and authentic respect for the roles each group played in the life of the church. To accomplish this, we relied on personal and communal inner work that animated our refusal to leave the table, carry out disagreements in the media, or engage in self-serving rhetoric of complaints and blaming.[55]

In other words, the "highest good" conceived by the LCWR spiritual imagination was not located at the pinnacle of a static hierarchy, but was found through the evolution of emerging relationships. Rightly ordered love leads to right relationships, indeed.

LCWR kept a posture of prophetic dialogue throughout the ordeal,[56] and the leadership describes their painful experience as "a sacred journey," whose "ultimate resolution benefitted everyone."[57] *However Long the Night: Making Meaning in a Time of Crisis* offers their account of the events, in a "serious effort to describe what LCWR's leaders learned personally and as an organization about how to weather a crisis in ways that create a new and better reality."[58] The LCWR leadership also expresses their hope:

> Our greatest desire now is that any positive outcome of these years of intense work at building relationships, establishing

---

53. Farrell, "Tapestry of Contrasting Colors," in Sanders, *However Long the Night*, 92.

54. Thompson, Regan, and Jelen, "Discovering Fresh Possibilities," in Sanders, *However Long the Night*, 148.

55. Allen and Deacon, "Relationships Matter," in Sanders, *However Long the Night*, 81.

56. See Mascarenhas, "Prophetic and Deliberative Responses."

57. LCWR, "Book Announcement."

58. LCWR, "Book Announcement."

> trust, inviting questions, and creating spaces for honest con-
> versations—even on topics that can be divisive—will serve as
> a source of hope to others within the church and the world.
> Clearly, such work is demanding and difficult, but in this age of
> intolerance of differences and growing polarities, it may be one
> of the most indispensable tasks of these times.[59]

By embodying integrity and humility in the midst of conflict, LCWR demonstrated the possibilities that open up when we imagine a horizon beyond
hierarchy. Indeed, their witness of humility, freedom, and joy offers "to the
world the true image of God."[60]

Johnson reminds us that this prophetic witness has been embodied
in women throughout church history. "Although women's words have been
censored or eliminated from much of Christian heritage," she writes, "in the
midst of these acts of exclusion, women have always been there, in fidelity
and struggle, in loving and caring, in outlawed movements, in prophecy and
vision."[61] These women dedicate their lives to Christ, and this, they understand, means being present with those who are poor and marginalized. It
means opening themselves to the vulnerability that love requires.

Farrell exhorts the church to embrace, honor, and incorporate this
female presence as we live into the future:

> Women Religious stand in very close proximity to people at the
> margins, to people with very painful, difficult situations in their
> lives. That is our gift to the church. Our gift to the church is to
> be with those who have been made poorer, with those on the
> margins. Questions there are much less black and white because
> human realities are much less black and white. That's where we
> spend our days. . . . A bishop, for instance, can't be on the street
> working with the homeless. He has other tasks. But we can be. So
> if there is a climate of open and trusting and adequate dialogue
> among us, we can bring together some of those conversations,
> and that's what I hope we can help develop in a deeper way.[62]

And Sister Simone Campbell, SSS, former executive director of NET-
WORK (a Catholic social justice lobby group that received a mention in
the CDF censure) concurs: "People ask where I get my courage, but it's not

59. Allen and Deacon, "Relationships Matter," in Sanders, *However Long the Night*,
81, citing "Statement of the LCWR Officers on the CDF Doctrinal Assessment and
Conclusion of the Mandate" (August 2015).

60. Francis, "Homily on Pentecost Sunday."

61. Johnson, *She Who Is*, 30.

62. Gross, "American Nun Responds."

courage, not really. When your heart's been broken, nothing can stop you. And living beside the poor, I had my heart broken every day. . . . When you are with the poor, really with the poor, you weep with them, you weep for the world. Weeping becomes part of your prayer."[63] Is this not where we find Christ?

PAUSE FOR REFLECTION

Take a moment to reflect on what you read.

- What is drawing your attention? What words, phrases, or concepts stand out to you? Are any new insights stirring in you?

- What does it mean to you that personhood is relational, and integrity requires vulnerability? Are there ways in which you resist this insight?

- How might your relationships be changed by adopting the paradigm of interconnection to which these women religious bear witness?

- Reflect on the poem, "Loaves and Fish," by Sister Simone Campbell, SSS:

> *I always joked*
> *that the miracle of loaves*
> *and fish was sharing.*
> *The women always knew this.*
> *But in this moment of need*
> *and notoriety, I ache, tremble*
> *almost weep at folks so*
> *hungry, malnourished,*
> *faced with spiritual famine*
> *of epic proportions. My heart*
> *aches with their need.*
> *Apostle like, I whine:*
> *"What are we among so many?"*

> *The consistent 2000-year-old*
> *ever-new response is this:*
> *"Blessed and broken, you are*
> *enough." I savor the blessed,*
> *cower at the broken and*
> *pray to be enough.*

63. Gordon, "Francis and the Nuns."

6

Centering Love at the Margins

An Evolutive Conversion

When we bear into the future the full knowledge of our past, we walk with hearts unfolded. We recognize the brutality of our species and as well the light in our spirits. We see that nothing is preserved, and no child or grandchild is saved, without brash acts of love and wild visions of continuance.

—Tiya Miles, *All That She Carried*

In July of 2012, after being notified of the CDF mandate, Pat Farrell, OSF, then-president of LCWR, observed in a newsletter column that the question of evolving community life and ministry shares a common thread with the question of responding to the doctrinal assessment:

> It occurs to me that what these two contexts and their questions have in common is the need for a deepening capacity to encounter "the other." "The other" might be voices of need we've not yet heard, [different partners in dialogue who can stretch our perspective toward unheard cries to which we're being called to respond], or persons whose mentalities make it difficult for us to find doors into effective dialogue. To meet "the other" as

the other really is, beyond our projections and resistance, is certainly a skill to be honed, but also a capability born in contemplative spaciousness. The ability to contemplate the other, to really see, takes us outside our habitual consciousness. . . . I believe it can carve out in us a deeper opening to God's presence in "the other."[1]

In light of the whole, that energy weaving together the community of being and drawing us all toward oneness, the other we have not met or acknowledged demands our attention as urgently as those we resist getting to know further. There is no "other" who falls outside the call to oneness. And when we encounter the other, we are graced with the presence of God.

Augustine, too, speaks of encountering God through interior spaciousness. "God," he senses, "is more interior to me than my most intimate intimacy."[2] And since our interior selves are enfolded within our relationships, the intimacy of interiority requires an expansive openness to encounter. We move "from the exterior to the interior"[3] and back again in our search for the whole.

As we encounter God, Augustine thinks, the truth will so delight our souls that we will relate to all of our loves holistically, justly. Though for him, our earthly loves become more authentic as we ascend the realms of the hierarchy of being, he recognizes that attending to the eternal will enable us to be present to other mortals despite the bounds of our humanity.

In a concise summary of his spirituality, Augustine tells us that "no one ought to be so leisured as to take no thought in that leisure for the interest of his [or her] neighbor, nor so active as to feel no need for the contemplation of God."[4] In other words, the soul that delights in truth will be rejuvenated through contemplative reflection; however, the love that develops in light of this truth should move us outward in encounter. Augustine's spiritual vision underscores the importance of traversing the confines of our limited experience to encounter the oneness beyond everything—but this must occur through encounter with others.

Channeling Augustine, Josephine Garrett, CSFN, writes that because "we understand God to be three distinct persons who are united and fully realized in the midst of their distinction . . . being made in the image and likeness of God includes a capacity and call to achieve communion with

1. Farrell, "Stay the Course."
2. Augustine, *Confessions*, III.6. (Translation in Desmond, "Companioning.")
3. Augustine, *Enarratio in Psalmum*, 145, as cited in Desmond, "Companioning."
4. Augustine, *City of God*, XIX.19.

one who is not me."[5] When we encounter others and allow their authentic being to inform our own sense of self, or our sense of the divine, we build our awareness of the whole.

This, of course, we do through Christ. Augustine emphasizes that "Christ is the starting point of your ascent and the goal of your ascent; you climb from [Christ's] example to [Christ's] divinity. [Christ] gave you an example by humbling [Christ-self]."[6] In this way, to encounter God, we must enter the depths of the "valley of tears," in which Christ is present. As Augustine admonishes, "Were we to forget that this must be our starting-point, we would be getting things upside down."[7] As though bearing witness to the wisdom of this claim, the leadership of LCWR recognizes that "perhaps more than any other constitutive element of our lives as religious, the practice of prayer helped us to be somewhat at peace with differences, polarization, and impasse. When there was no clear way forward, the only way was down, in surrender to the presence at the core of each of us and within all of reality."[8]

But if we take our starting point as the incarnate Christ, then our pursuit of God should be reordered on a horizontal plane—forgetting our starting point in Christ would be to get things sideways, not upside down. Christ's participation in the evolving, interconnected cosmos, and Christ's humble identification with those suffering in the "valley of tears," points toward accompaniment and encounter, rather than metaphysical ascent, as the path for seeking God. And insofar as we open ourselves to the vulnerability of encounter, we walk in the footsteps of the incarnate Christ. Here, the vertical and horizontal dimensions of faith merge.

SEEING THE OTHER: A BIG "IF"

Delio notes that Jesus of Nazareth's "message was one of bold vision, reflected in his frequent use of words such as *behold, look, see*—'the kingdom of heaven is among you' (Luke 17:21). To see is an act of consciousness; it brings what is seen into conscious reality. Jesus's desire to see required an open heart. It was not simply to 'take a look'; rather, he called his disciples to gaze, to have an inner spaciousness of the heart to receive another into it."[9] The kingdom of heaven is here, unfolding toward the future; we need only

5. Garrett, "Martin Luther King Jr."
6. Augustine, *Essential Expositions*, 119.1.
7. Augustine, *Essential Expositions*, 120.1.
8. Farrell, "Tapestry of Contrasting Colors," in Sanders, *However Long the Night*, 92.
9. Delio, *Making All Things New*, 72.

to look, to open ourselves to the reality of wholeness. And this entails, especially, encountering those on the margins. As Pope Francis observes, "You have to go to the edges of existence if you want to see the world as it is."[10]

Although Augustine's spiritual vision was one focused upward, it is conceptually helpful as we develop a paradigm to help us expand our horizons. Augustine describes his first vision of the One as an "instant of awe," in which, he writes, "my mind attained to the sight of the God who is. Then, at last, I caught sight of your invisible nature, as it is known through your creatures."[11] We see this emphasis on sight, too, in his mystical experience in Ostia with Monica, his mother. After describing the way in which all of creation is enfolded in a whole beyond itself, Augustine wonders what it would be like if "this single vision entranced and absorbed the one who beheld it and enveloped him [or her] in inward joys in such a way that for him [or her] life was eternally the same as that instant of understanding for which we had longed so much."[12]

As Augustine attains to the sight of God, he catches a glimpse of creation with the eyes of eternal energy—he is able to appreciate the unity-in-diversity that is the absolute wholeness of being. Augustine, here, offers a cosmological understanding of oneness: the One is not to be found apart from created beings, but enfolds all that is, together in love. Arthur Ledoux articulates Augustine's compelling insight thus:

> For us to see the world the way God sees it is to touch on nothing less than mystical union with God. When our self becomes fully open to and aligned with God's perspective, we seem to become transparent. . . . Our situation is much deeper than we thought it was; we thought we were seeing and loving the things of nature. In fact, God is seeing and loving God's self through us. To be an open pathway for such seeing and loving is, Augustine thinks, to participate in the inner life of the Trinity and to have a foretaste of the beatific vision in paradise.[13]

And the humility of Christ serves as the paradigm of the beatific vision—without it, we cannot view the world with the perspective of a finite participant in the whole.

Importantly, Christ's identification with the most marginalized of society serves to unify the start and end points of our faith journey—"the starting point and goal"—just as Augustine envisioned: marginalization entails

10. Francis and Ivereigh, *Let Us Dream*, 11.

11. Augustine, *Confessions*, VII.17.

12. Augustine, *Confessions*, IX.10.

13. Ledoux, "Green Augustine," 335.

being pushed to the outer edges, and our pursuit of God must start there; but as we centralize encounters with those who have been marginalized, our horizons continuously expand through inclusive encounter. Rightly ordered love moves outward in encounter and back inward in self-awareness in an ever-expanding cycle toward the fullness of being, encompassed by oneness.

An oft-cited (if misrepresented) passage in the Gospels offers helpful insights into this line of thought: When a woman pours a jar of expensive perfume over Jesus, the disciples wonder whether the perfume could have been better used by selling it and giving the money to the poor; Jesus tells them in response, "the poor will always be with you, but me you will not always have with you."[14]

It is tempting to read this passage as an excuse to turn our eyes from the margins toward the heavens. Isn't Jesus, here, affirming a hierarchy of truth and being, telling us that it is more important to worship him than to empower neighbors who are poor? But reading this through the lens of interconnection, we can get a sense of what it might mean to encounter Christ in the flesh through persons who have been marginalized—or what it means to transcend our limited view of reality and evolve our consciousness toward wholeness.

Augustine's reflection on Jesus's claim that the poor will always be here glosses over the first clause: "What [Jesus] has thus said is true. When were the poor wanting in the Church?" Augustine asks this rhetorically before moving on to examine the second clause, in which he finds reason for the church to welcome all to the Eucharistic table—even "thieves and infidels."[15]

He interprets Jesus's words to mean that "now you have Christ, but by living wickedly you will not have [Christ] always."[16] And what does it mean to live wickedly? As we learned in previous chapters, it means to cling to a limited good as though it were the whole; to assert yourself in pride rather than humble yourself in love, which hastens to empower those in need.[17] An Augustinian interpretation thus recognizes that Christ compels us to remain ever open—with hands and hearts—to those who are made poor,[18] and to avoid excluding others, deeming them unworthy of encounter. Christ exhorts us to be facilitators of wholeness. And importantly, Christ is the mediator that embodies wholeness and enables us to attend to the whole.

14. Matt 26:11.

15. Augustine, *Tractates*, 50.12.

16. Augustine, *Tractates*, 50.12.

17. Augustine, *Love One Another*, 52.

18. We must remember, too, that there are many different types of poverty. I have written about what I call "poverty of influence" in Bonnette, "Oscar Romero."

There is more to be said about this passage, though. Jesus was, once again, identifying himself with those who are poor: you will not always have *me*, we might understand him to say, but I will be present with you, especially in those who are suffering. Perhaps Christ is commending us to the embrace of those on the margins: the whole is enfolded in Christ's body, which is encompassed most fully in the life of persons who are poor. The woman who poured perfume recognized that in loving the particular body of Jesus, which would bear the marks of human suffering, she could love the whole despite her finitude.

The key to the whole vignette, though, I think, is that Jesus's words were spoken in reference to Deuteronomy 15, with which the disciples would have been familiar. In that passage, God commands the people to give to one another generously, forgiving debts and sharing with those in need. We read that since God "will bless you abundantly in the land . . . there shall be no one of you in need if you but listen to the voice of the Lord, your God, and carefully observe this entire commandment which I enjoin on you today."[19] A few verses later, however, we find the reality check: "The land will never lack for needy persons."[20] In other words, "the poor" will always be with us precisely because we do not embody the openness required for genuine community.[21]

I recently heard this insight repackaged for our time. In a panel discussion reflecting on the life and legacy of Servant of God Thea Bowman, FSPA, Patricia Chappell, SNDdeN, who serves on the leadership team for the Sisters of Notre Dame de Namur US East-West Province and formerly served as President of the National Black Sisters' Conference, was asked, "How do we continue the work [of Sister Thea]?" Her emphatic response is worth quoting at length:

> Structures will change when the value systems that uphold and keep racism alive in those structures change. When we look at all of the social systems in the U.S., they mirror Eurocentric values . . . based in either/or thinking, a focus on scarcity, a model of secrecy, and individual action and/or competition. Those values are basically what have formed the foundation of our social systems, including our beloved Institutional Catholic Church. And so what has happened is systemic racism has been embedded in every single one of our social systems, including the Catholic Church. And those social systems, my brothers

19. Deut 15:4–5.
20. Deut 15:11.
21. I was inspired in this line of thinking by reading Clark, "Ignorant Christians."

and sisters, they work: they maintain an organization; they keep things moving; they keep things efficient. But those same systems are what continue to be the boot on the neck of marginalized, oppressed, and black and brown communities. If we want to build an inclusive and just Beloved Community, then we have to create a new paradigm; we have to begin to reimagine; and we have to begin to form "transformational values," which need to be the core of our structures and institutions. Those transformational values and/or antiracist values include not either/or thinking, but both/and thinking; not looking at something from a scarcity worldview, but taking it all in from an abundant worldview; beginning to look at transparent communication, not models of secrecy, which has gotten us in so much mess in the church as we have it; and let's move away from individual action and let's talk about collaboration and networking. It seems to me that when we can begin to do that, we will begin to build an anti-racist, multicultural Catholic Church. But I warn you, it is a big "if"! Because it means that folks are going to have to give up white privilege and white power. And that is not anti-Gospel: it is very much part of our Catholic social teachings, but we have to be willing to go there. And my concern is that we sometimes come off as scared Christians or scared Catholics because we don't want to go there.[22]

She concludes with this challenge: "We have to change the paradigm! The paradigm has got to shift if we're going to be bringing about the Beloved Church and the Beloved Community, which I believe we all long for."[23] *If* we can adopt a new paradigm, one based on interconnection and humility, rather than individualism and pride, "there shall be no one in need"—the kin-dom of God will be at hand.

Without making room for new levels of consciousness, without expanding our moral vision through authentic encounters, without being willing to "go there," our love quickly turns to the grasping, oppressive love that Augustine warns us is deceptively harmful, and we cannot move toward truth. Instead, we should keep a posture of humility so that our love can "open wide the hand of the soul"[24] and foster the interconnection that is the reality of our being.

22. Chappell, in Georgetown University, "Sister Thea Bowman," 46:06. (Lightly edited for length and clarity.)

23. Chappell, in Georgetown University, "Sister Thea Bowman," 46:06. (Lightly edited for length and clarity.)

24. Schlabach, "'Love is the Hand,'" 1.

As we consider what a paradigm shift might entail, Augustine's description of encountering God is instructive: "Let us picture to ourselves a man or woman called to make the ascent. Where will it take place? In the heart. What is the starting point? Humility, the valley of weeping. Whither is he [or she] to ascend? To a reality that cannot be put into words. . . . *To the place God has appointed.*"[25] The heart, the organ of love, is that which moves us; the starting point must be among those who have been made poor and marginalized—our hearts must draw us to their side, to the valley of weeping; the place God has appointed is what the world is evolving toward, a reality that cannot be put into words: oneness, or wholeness.[26]

JUDGING THE OTHER: OPENNESS OR RELATIVISM?

To evolve toward wholeness, we must look to the edges of existence—to those who have been excluded, marginalized, or otherwise made poor—and reach out to accompany them. But more importantly, we must make room for those who have been marginalized to accompany us, remaining open to their insights even, and perhaps especially, when they challenge "traditional" ideals.

The Congregation for the Doctrine of the Faith (CDF) tells us that from the "sacramentality [of the community of the Body of Christ] it follows that the Church is not a reality closed in on herself; rather, she is permanently open to missionary and ecumenical endeavour, for she is sent to the world to announce and witness, to make present and spread the mystery of communion which is essential to her: to gather together all people and all things into Christ."[27] But as Gebara remarks, "At times I wonder if the questions of traditional theology have any meaning for the poor, and for 'the poor' here means eighty percent of the population."[28] And Pope Francis echoes this sentiment, claiming, persons who are poor "always and everywhere, evangelize us, because they enable us to discover in new ways the true face" of God.[29] When we look for Christ in others first, we discover new aspects of love.

In Matthew's version of the Great Commission, Christ extolls his followers to go and make disciples, "baptizing them in the name of the [Trinity]

25. Augustine, *Essential Expositions*, 119.2. Emphasis in original.
26. See John 17:20–26.
27. CDF, "Letter to the Bishops."
28. Cited in Puelo, *Struggle Is One*, 209.
29. Francis, "Message."

and teaching them to observe all that I have commanded you." Of course, the greatest commandment, according to Jesus, is this: "You shall love the Lord, your God, with all your heart, with all your soul, and with all your mind. . . . The second is like it: You shall love your neighbor as yourself."[30]

The word Jesus uses for *like* when he says, "the second is like it," is the same word he uses when he begins a parable: 'The kingdom of heaven is *like* . . .' In this light, love of self and neighbor can be understood as love of the whole, put in contexts we limited creatures can understand and embody. Rather than proposing a vertical/horizontal dichotomy, might Jesus, here, be affirming the finite particularities of human love, the local relationships through which we express our love of the whole?

In other words, as we adopt a paradigm of wholeness and interconnection, "making disciples" becomes less about convincing others to conform to our view and more about encountering the other in a space of humility. This interpretation garners support when Jesus issues "a new commandment: love one another. As I have loved you, so you also should love one another. This is how all will know that you are my disciples: if you have love for one another."[31] Surely, love will point others toward wholeness—it cannot be unconcerned with the wellbeing of the other. And yet, love always should start with openness, with a willingness to see the other as the other really is and to learn what the other has to teach.

This is one reason why, as Isasi-Díaz argues, "The church has to be a church of the impoverished and oppressed, not a church for them, which is a church where they have no say in creating its meaning."[32] But this, she writes, "requires a radical change in church structures, structures that privilege the church's hierarchies, its ministers, and those theologians recognized by church authorities. To radically affirm the option [for the poor] requires from the church a willingness to consider radically changing how it understands itself and its relationship to the kin-dom of God."[33]

As we have seen, the hierarchical paradigm of order that has informed our theology plays into the *libido dominandi* and tempts the church to seek domination rather than encounter. As Jamie T. Phelps, OP, observes, "We have confused preaching the gospel with self-aggrandizing leadership and posturing in the pulpit, ecclesial meetings, and gatherings."[34] To preach the

30. Matt 22:37–39.

31. John 13:34–35.

32. Isasi-Díaz, "Mujerista Discourse," in Isasi-Díaz and Mendieta, *Decolonizing Epistemologies*, 67.

33. Isasi-Díaz, "Mujerista Discourse," in Isasi-Díaz and Mendieta, *Decolonizing Epistemologies*, 66.

34. Phelps, "Communion Ecclesiology," in Copeland, *Uncommon Faithfulness*, 120.

Gospel is, rather, to accompany persons who are poor and marginalized in practical love, and to pray, with Christ, that all will be one, trusting that the grace of the Spirit will draw us all toward wholeness.

Insofar as static cosmologies and hierarchical worldviews have fossilized the way we think about God or have caused us to dismiss the insights of those who challenge our perceptions, they have closed us in on ourselves—we have made idols out of our ideals. To live in authentic community, to attain the joy of beatific vision, we must reorient our loves to be ever more expansive. Through Jesus's embodied love, Copeland argues, "the covenantal community was changed and renewed with the presence and potential participation of bodies formerly absent, and experienced an inflow of hope and joy."[35] The church as the Body of Christ must reflect this inclusive sense of the whole.

Some years ago, just after earning my doctorate in theology, I was asked to give a lecture on the relationship between love and justice in Augustine's thought. I described with charismatic conviction the connection between rightly ordered love and right relationships, asserting that ascending to God in love should manifest in action for justice, and emphasizing that without the constraint of this order of love, our actions would be motivated by the *libido dominandi* and thus would fall short of fostering relationships that were *right*. It had not occurred to me yet that it might matter who was defining the order.

Afterward, I was approached by a young woman, who introduced herself as a Catholic, a graduate student of theology, a campus minister at her university, and a lesbian. She asked what I would say to the LGBTQ+ community, who are told by the Institutional Catholic Church that the expression of their love is "intrinsically disordered"[36]—what might right relationships look like for them?

My response was simplistic. I conflated a specific application of the social teaching of the church with eternal truth and reminded her charitably that ordering our lives according to truth is meant to be for our own flourishing. Her eyes, resigned, held the hurt of a wound torn open yet again, as she graciously but pointedly asked, "Shouldn't our human experience have something to offer orthodoxy?" Her question stayed with me, and although I did not realize it at the time, her witness moved me along in this theological and spiritual journey.

Indeed, now I would respond with a resounding "Yes!" Of course experience should inform our sense of truth—not that it should define it,

35. Copeland, *Enfleshing Freedom*, 61.
36. See CCC §2357.

but if we are to form our spirits according to a sense of the whole, it is crucial that our faith tradition be infused with the wisdom acquired from all walks of life, especially from those who have been marginalized and made vulnerable.

Thea Bowman bore witness to this when she urged the church to "work together so that all of us have equal access to input—equal access to opportunity—equal access to participation. Go in the room and look around and see who's missing and send some of your folk out to call them in so that the church can be what she claims to be—truly Catholic."[37] If people have been excluded from the table, we should actively seek them out to learn from them. Without listening to the voices of the *other*, we close ourselves off to the "true truth,"[38] as Bowman would say, which we get at only through inclusive interconnection, wholeness, and love.

Importantly, though, we must also be willing to ask how the church can help us to become more open, even if its teaching runs counter to our experience. Though I do not need to grapple with the alienation generated by church teaching that calls my way of loving "intrinsically disordered," I do feel this tension personally when it comes to the church's prohibition on the use of contraception.

My husband and I practice Natural Family Planning (NFP), and for the most part, this has been a gift. I am glad to forego introducing unnecessary hormones into my body or contributing to plastic pollution when there is a natural, waste-free way to monitor fertility and avoid pregnancy. But when I do want to avoid pregnancy, what happens if that natural way is not an option? Must we deny our sexuality for the good of our souls?

For a year after each of my children was born, while I was chasing toddlers by day and nursing a newborn by night, my menstrual cycle was elusive. This meant that every sexual encounter with my husband brought with it intense worry that we had slept together during an unperceived ovulation, which could result in another pregnancy. Though such an outcome was unlikely, it was not impossible, and exacerbated by lack of sleep and post-partum hormones, the mental stress became overwhelming. Eventually we would decide to abstain until it became possible to monitor symptoms again.

But often, in the craziness of life with little ones, reaching for each other after collapsing into bed at night is the only opportunity to express intimacy. I struggled profoundly with the rule that we could not use contraception even temporarily, as though openness to life in a marriage is defined solely

37. Bowman, "Sr. Thea Bowman's Address."
38. Cited in Danielewicz, "Thea Bowman & Bede Abram."

by childbearing, and not by nurturing the lives already present in our family or community. Indeed, being open to life was the very reason it would have been unwise to become pregnant again, since my body was healing from the birth of a child and my little ones needed me to be available to care for them, not curled up on the bathroom floor with morning sickness. It did not make any sense to me. It still does not.

And certainly, I recognize the privilege of being able to practice NFP at all: I have a husband who respects my "no" and partners with me to raise our children; a steady income that could support another child if I misread the chart; and a body strong enough to sustain another pregnancy. Many women are denied these privileges, and if they refuse contraception, their wellbeing will be compromised in practical and visceral ways; but using contraception, they are told, will jeopardize their souls. What are they do to?

Did my husband and I choose correctly when we denied the physical expression of our love, for the sake of something beyond our understanding? I am reminded of Adam's choice to eat with Eve, limiting his capacity to love wholeness itself for the sake of accompanying his beloved. Can we do otherwise? Should we?

By wrestling with church teaching with an open spirit, even when it seems to run counter to our desires, we can gain important insights into what will facilitate wholeness, as we bring our own experiences to bear on its interpretation. Chastity, for example, is an important virtue. It teaches us to enfold the gift of our bodies within the gift of our minds—to avoid physical risk behaviors and to view our partners as people to be loved rather than things to serve our needs. And as we have seen from the witness of women religious, it can also offer a strong statement of bodily autonomy and personal dignity. In marriage, avoiding contraception can be a helpful tool for cultivating chastity, just as heterosexual love offers an immediately obvious means of being open to life. But these are not the only ways to foster these virtues or express such openness.

It is worth noting that renowned biblical scholar Walter Brueggemann—in a piece in which he describes the need for Christians to adjudicate the tension between biblical *texts of rigor* concerning LGBTQ+ persons, such as Leviticus 18:22; 20:13; Deuteronomy 23:1; and Romans 1:23–27, and *texts of welcome*, such as those found in Isaiah 56; Matthew 11:28–30; Galatians 3:28; and Acts 10—recognizes that "the struggle to maintain the identity and the 'purity' of the holy people of God was always a matter of dispute and contention."[39] Further, he argues, "we do our interpretive work

39. Brueggemann, "How to Read the Bible."

in a context that is, in general ways, impacted by and shaped through this struggle for what is old and what is new."[40] He writes,

> Each of us, as interpreter, has a specific context. But we can say something quite general about our shared interpretive context. It is evident that Western culture (and our place in it) is at a decisive point wherein we are leaving behind many old, long-established patterns of power and meaning, and we are observing the emergence of new patterns of power and meaning. It is not difficult to see our moment as an instance anticipated by the prophetic poet:
>
> Do not remember the former things, or consider the things of old. I am about to do a new thing; now it springs forth, do you not perceive it? (Is. 43:18–19)
>
> The "old things" among us have long been organized around white male power, with its tacit, strong assumption of heterosexuality, plus a strong accent on American domination. The "new thing" emerging among us is a multiethnic, multicultural, multiracial, multi-gendered culture in which old privileges and positions of power are placed in deep jeopardy.
>
> We can see how our current politico-cultural struggles (down to the local school board) have to do with resisting what is new and protecting and maintaining what is old or, conversely, welcoming what is new with a ready abandonment of what is old.
>
> If this formulation from Isaiah roughly fits our circumstance in Western culture, then we can see that the *texts of welcome* are appropriate to our "new thing," while the *texts of rigor* function as a defense of what is old. . . .
>
> In the rhetoric of Jesus, this new arrival may approximate among us the "coming of the kingdom of God," except that the coming kingdom is never fully here but is only "at hand," and we must not overestimate the arrival of newness.[41]

As we have seen, authentic relationships are impossible when we are turned inward, focused only on what seems right to us; the church helps to point us to a reality beyond ourselves. However, to the degree that the church has interpreted its theology without input from those on the margins—especially those who are non-white, non-male, and non-heterosexual—it, too, suffers from an inward turn, which can lead to emphasizing rigor over welcome. Theologian MT Dávila writes, "the preferential option [for the poor] inherently orients discipleship toward the marginalized and

---

40. Brueggemann, "How to Read the Bible."
41. Brueggemann, "How to Read the Bible."

victimized other and her or his life experiences, and yet a culture of privilege turns the person inordinately toward the self."[42] To follow Christ, we must be willing to look to those who have been marginalized and listen to their wisdom; and we must be open to the possibility that our sense of right is limited. Participating in dialogue through encounter can lift up shared wisdom and can help us acknowledge the choices we make as we struggle with the vulnerability and uncertainty of human existence—our limited capacity to express our love.

This openness cannot come from clinging to abstract moral absolutes, and though the church has come to be associated with such abstractions, our tradition asks us to bring our moral theology down to a practical level. As Brueggemann puts it, "We are thus required to come to terms with the 'other,' who disturbs our reductionist management of life through sameness. We have a fairly simple choice that can refer to the other as a threat, a rival enemy, a competitor, or we may take the other as a neighbor."[43] If God is the energy of love drawing us toward the whole, then our participation in that energy is not ordered by static absolutes, but by community. And if our community has been exclusionary, it cannot be just; if we are evolving, so too should our moral consciousness. "In many specific ways," Brueggemann suggests, "our cultural conflicts—and the decisions we must make—reverberate with the big issue of God's coming newness."[44]

Often, we adherents of tradition resist attempts to reconcile the old codes—the rigorist interpretations—with new experience, believing ourselves and the church bound by them, despite the fact that, as Brueggemann explains, "the Bible does not speak with a single voice on any topic. Inspired by God as it is, all sorts of persons have a say in the complexity of Scripture, and we are under mandate to listen, as best we can, to all of its voices."[45]

Consider, for example, Saint Pope John Paul II's declaration that "the Church has no authority whatsoever to confer priestly ordination on women and that this judgment is to be definitively held by all the Church's faithful."[46] We read in the Gospel that Peter was given the keys to the kingdom of heaven, and Augustine reminds us that we know what it means to hold these keys: "Whatever you bind on earth shall be bound in heaven, and whatever you loose on earth shall be loosed in heaven."[47] But Augustine tells

42. Dávila, "Challenge."
43. Brueggemann, "How to Read the Bible."
44. Brueggemann, "How to Read the Bible."
45. Brueggemann, "How to Read the Bible."
46. John Paul II, *Ordinatio Sacerdotalis*, §4.
47. Matt 18:18. See Augustine, Sermon 229N, 2, in Augustine, *Essential Sermons*.

us that Peter was not the only recipient: "I make bold to say, we too have these keys. And what am I to say? That it is only we who bind, only we who loose? No, you also bind, you also loose."[48] Peter, Augustine thinks, stands for the whole church, in its unity.[49]

Though habit (or tradition) is a powerful constraint, we, the whole church, are called to loose what needs to be loosened to promote the flourishing and participation of all in the community of being. As Augustine puts it movingly, "Look at Lazarus's case; he came out, all tied up. . . . What does the Church do, told as it has been, *Whatever you loose shall be loosed*? What the Lord went on at once to tell the disciples, of course: *Unbind him and let him go*."[50] We cannot justify our moral claims with reference to an absolute ideal, since the absolute is mystery and ideals must be embodied. Rather, we must discover and work out what is right through expansive encounter.

Often, our moral convictions inhibit this kind of authentic encounter. Wary of moral relativism, we might wonder what will serve as a moral compass if we are always to be discovering and discerning. So we hem ourselves in, unwilling to learn from those who challenge our convictions. Doctrinal concerns color our relationships and prevent us from truly seeing the other.

But perhaps we avoid relativism less by clinging to our interpretation of absolute truth, and more by remaining open to new perspectives. If relativism is the failure to acknowledge an eternal order of love, maintaining instead our personal convictions as arbitrary prerogatives, then ethical interpretations that are not open to the order of the whole are, themselves, relativistic. Certainly, relativism is dangerous: if we attend only to what we ourselves feel is right or good, we feed into our lust for domination by closing ourselves off to the whole. But to have integrity, to live authentically, we have to be willing to encounter others in humility. Finding God, and developing corresponding moral sensibilities, requires us to turn our eyes outward and then to grapple with the implications of that encounter for our interior lives. In the continuous evolution generated by encounter and conversion, we grow closer to the wholeness of being that energizes the world.

Augustine might seem an unlikely source for this kind of ethic, but when he is at his most vulnerable, we can sense his struggle to balance his pastoral responsibilities with his worry that he might, in fact, be leading his flock astray. "I do your bidding in word and deed alike," he writes: "I do it beneath the protection of your wings, for the peril would be too great if it

---

48. Augustine, Sermon 229N, 2, in Augustine, *Essential Sermons*.

49. Augustine, Sermon 229N, 2, in Augustine, *Essential Sermons*.

50. Augustine, Sermon 67, 3, in Augustine, *Sermons*. See John 11:44. I am indebted to Allan Fitzgerald on this point.

were not that my soul has submitted to you and sought the shelter of your wings and that my weakness is known to you."[51] This is not as pessimistic as it might seem; it rather indicates his very human concern that his efforts to direct the church toward God might be misguided, and a recognition that it is grace that moves us along, evolving us toward wholeness.

Contemplating what it will mean to know God in the whole, Augustine offers insight into what it means to make judgments with limited human perspective:

> Perhaps God will be known to us and visible to us in the sense that [God] will be spiritually perceived by each one of us in each one of us, perceived in one another, perceived by each in himself [or herself]; [God] will be seen in the new heaven and the new earth, in the whole creation as it then will be; [God] will be seen in every body by means of bodies, wherever the eyes of the spiritual body are directed with their penetrating gaze. The thoughts of our minds will lie open to mutual observation; and the words of the Apostle will be fulfilled; for he said, "Pass no premature judgments," adding immediately, "until the Lord comes. For [Christ] will light up what is hidden in darkness and will reveal the thoughts of the heart."

When we conceive of God, we are always doing so out of our personal experiences—our spiritual vision is limited; there are truths hidden beyond the boundaries of our perception. We cannot attain the fullness of truth unless we transcend our limitations through relational encounters and perceive love evolving through the whole of creation. As Diana L. Hayes reminds us, "theology emerges from a people's efforts to understand themselves in relation to God. Yet God is always and everywhere incomprehensible mystery. As St. Augustine realized, if we have understood, then what we have understood is not God."[52]

In this light, the critique offered by Clara Sue Kidwell, Homer Noley, and George E. Tinker regarding Native American experience bears important weight:

> If the . . . Christ is merely that aspect of God that communicates creativity and healing or salvation to human beings, then Indian people can contribute to Christianity's knowledge of salvation from our own experiences and memories of God's functioning among Indian communities throughout our history. . . . But [this] means that we can never be trapped into saying that God

51. Augustine, *Confessions*, X.4.
52. Hayes, *And Still We Rise*, 1.

has only spoken this good news through Jesus, or that the only
way to salvation is through a Euro-western message brought by
the colonizer to the conquered.[53]

Mary Hughes, OP, puts it well: "Each of these [cultural] realities are merely different and contribute to the wonderful diversity that is humankind.
The inherent danger is that one can come to believe that one's way of being is the only way, the best way, or the right way. . . . Such diversity can
enrich the church immeasurably. However, such diverse experiences also
hold the potential for conflict and misunderstanding."[54] And so, Kidwell,
Noley, and Tinker ask a question with which Western Christians must
grapple: "Why should Indian people be coerced to give up God's unique
self disclosure to us?"[55]

Are we willing to encounter the other in a space of humility, to learn
what God has communicated to them without immediately dismissing their
insights? Are we willing to call all to the table? Sharon Holland, IHM, observes the dangers and difficulty of encountering others from a position of
moral certitude: "A part of our difficulty seems to be that we are not even
aware of the chasm or, perhaps, that we are seeing only our perceived reality.
We know our truth and do not understand that it is not what is perceived by
the other. We accept what we perceive of the other as fact, without considering if that is the other's perception as well. . . . We may say that no one is
really seeing or hearing."[56]

A desire to discover truth cannot be satisfied by anything less than
continuous dialectical engagement—and even in this, we will not "arrive" at
truth but must find satisfaction in the pursuit of it. Since, Augustine tells us,
"falsehood consists in not living in the way for which [we were] created,"[57]
we humans, dust of the earth, imbued with consciousness, must find truth
through encounter—through expanding moral vision toward the whole
that enfolds us, through and toward which we are evolving.

This is why, as Phelps reminds us, Jesus's proclamation of the kingdom
of God "essentially aimed to open the minds and hearts of those within the
religious community and the dominant society to establish patterns of human and cosmological relationships resonant with those envisioned by God
at the dawn of creation and made possible only by God's self-gift of grace."[58]

53. Kidwell et al., *Native American Theology*, 78.

54. Hughes, "Spiritual Journey," in Sanders, *However Long the Night*, 120.

55. Kidwell et al., *Native American Theology*, 83.

56. Holland, "Power of Secrecy," in Sanders, *However Long the* Night, 114.

57. Augustine, *City of God*, XIV.4.

58. Phelps, "Communion Ecclesiology," in Copeland, *Uncommon Faithfulness*, 118.

Cosmological consciousness thus unites the immanent and the transcendent: God is the fullness of evolution—the whole of all actual and potential existence, found in each being now, but fully in the kin-dom of God, the experience of right relationships graced by love.

We cannot hope to order our love rightly if it is directed vertically toward a static absolute; instead, the order of the cosmos is one of evolutive interconnection and so, too, should be our pursuit of God. Thus, as Phelps encourages, the life of the church "must be directed toward realizing the continuance of the mission of Jesus Christ expressed in his vision of liberating oppressed people from debilitating economic and spiritual poverty, mental and physical imprisonment, and moral and intellectual blindness. In all our efforts we must honor the fullness of humanity of all peoples and strive to bring about the unity of the human community with all creation."[59]

Only by orienting our sense of the real and the true toward an ever-expansive horizon can we begin to apprehend, and embody, the wholeness of the One. The call to "go and make disciples" cannot be read through the lens of static hierarchy. Rather, the gospel we are called to proclaim is the good news of oneness; of openness, humility, and interconnection; of evolutive emergence; of relationships baptized in the unity-in-diversity of the Triune God.

By encountering the *other*, we encounter God; by loving the world, we evolve toward wholeness.

LOVING THE OTHER: ACTING JUSTLY[60]

So how can we act with the courage of conviction, if we remain open to conversion? Shifting our paradigm from one of hierarchy to one of interconnection mitigates the apparent tension between these two. If our convictions are grounded in humility and ordered toward the wholeness of being, then they orient us toward openness, and the measure we use to determine what is right becomes the flourishing of the poor and marginalized.

It is worth noting that this is not a radically new claim: Catholic social teaching insists that those who are vulnerable and marginalized in society deserve our special concern. We should remember, however, that flourishing must be judged not simply according to traditional precepts, which have been colored by exclusion, but according to the vision of those on the

---

59. Phelps, "Communion Ecclesiology," in Copeland, *Uncommon Faithfulness*, 120.

60. I developed some of the themes in this section previously in Bonnette, "No Surprise" and "Catholics: Embrace Being 'Woke.'"

margins. A paradigm of interconnection turns us toward encounter and helps us recognize our limits in the vast expanse of human experience.

We begin by seeing, by ensuring that our convictions are formed in light of encounter. We can ask questions such as: Whom have I ignored? Whose experience have I failed to acknowledge? Whose voice am I listening to right now? Is it one that encourages me to look outside of myself and my own convictions? Is it one that is calling forth exclusion or inclusion? What are those who are poor and marginalized calling for at this time? Am I allowing my own privilege to limit my moral vision?

And when we act on our convictions, do we notice them fostering unity and inclusion, or generating discord? Does dissent come from those with power and privilege, or from those on the margins? Augustine writes, "You can test the truth of what you are singing only if you are beginning to act in harmony with your song."[61] We can test the truth of our convictions only when we see the actual effects that they produce—and if the effects are divisive or exclusive, if they privilege the powerful, then our song is off-key.

In political life, urgent needs require urgent action, but we know that even our best efforts will have negative implications for some. Making policy choices in a way that prioritizes the full participation of the marginalized— human and nonhuman—will move us further toward wholeness. And when we decide on a course of action, we must look again toward those who have been or may be harmed to learn how we might facilitate their flourishing, as well. The transformational values of both/and thinking and a mindset of abundance can guide us, here.

Helpfully, Augustine recognizes that, at times, it can be difficult to discern the responsibilities we have toward others, and moving outward in love can be challenging. He writes:

> All [people] are to be loved equally. But since you cannot do good to all, you are to pay special regard to those who, by the accidents of time, or place, or circumstance, are brought into closer connection with you. For, suppose that you had a great deal of some commodity, and felt bound to give it away to somebody who had none, and that it could not be given to more than one person; if two persons presented themselves, neither of whom had either from need or relationship a greater claim upon you than the other, you could do nothing fairer than choose by lot to which you would give what could not be given to both. Just so among [people]: since you cannot consult for the good of them all, you must take the matter as decided for you by a sort

61. Augustine, *Essential Expositions*, 119.9.

of lot, according as each [person] happens for the time being to be more closely connected with you.[62]

Augustine thus helps to ease the conceptual tension that arises when the entire cosmos is seen to make moral claims upon us. Appreciating our finitude while remaining open to the transcendent whole is key to actualizing our loves. But again, we have to acknowledge the shortcomings of even our most just choices and try to find ways to mitigate the inequity.

If our human limitations prevent us from actually succeeding in right relationships, that is no reason not to try. As Augustine puts it, "By the gift of grace [one] is not only shown how to see you . . . but is also given the strength to hold you. By your grace, too, if [someone] is far from you and cannot see you, [he or she] is enabled to walk upon the path that leads [him or her] closer to you, so that [he or she] may see you and hold you."[63] Indeed, taking a cosmological perspective reminds us that in the trying, we further (or hinder) the earth's evolution toward wholeness, as well as our own.

Brink's reflection on a dialogue between Peter and Jesus offers helpful insights, here. As you read, bear in mind Augustine's injunction, "When you hear the Lord saying Peter, do you love me? Think of it as a mirror, and observe yourself there. . . . What else was Peter doing but standing for the Church?"[64]

> Three times Jesus asks Peter if he loves him. We see this as parallel to the three times Peter denied Jesus. But what may escape our notice is the vocabulary that Jesus uses. When we look at the words for "love" in the Greek text, we appreciate more fully the encounter between Jesus and Peter.
>
> Jesus asks Peter if he loves him the first time, and uses the verbal form of the word *agapē*: "Peter, do you *agapē* me more than these?" Peter responds, "Yes, Lord, you know that I *philō* you." Jesus is asking of Peter that type of love that lays down one's life for one's friend, the type of love that God has of us, an expansive love. That's *agapē*. Peter responds that he holds a friendship love, *philō*—one based on doing good, reciprocating and working toward the betterment of the friend. Again Jesus asks Peter, "Do you *agapē* me?" Peter doesn't hear the distinction. He responds, "You know that I *philō* you." The third time Jesus asks, "Peter do you *philō* me?" And Peter responds, "You know that I *philō* you." Jesus changes his vocabulary. Peter is

62. Augustine, *On Christian Doctrine*, I.28.29.

63. Augustine, *Confessions*, VII.21.

64. Augustine, Sermon 229N, 2, in Augustine, *Essential Sermons*.

not yet ready to love as Jesus desires. Nonetheless, Jesus entrusts him with the care of the community, recognizing that friendship love leads to the kind of love that God asks of all God's children: *agapē*.[65]

We all struggle to love perfectly, but Christ enfolds our imperfect efforts into fullness of being. The key is to make the effort, acknowledge the lack, and try again.

This has become clear to me as I have tried to respond to Pope Francis's call for ecological conversion, which echoes that of Saint Pope John Paul II.[66] Francis, recognizing that "the earth herself, burdened and laid waste, is among the most abandoned and maltreated of our poor,"[67] exhorts Christians to embrace an "'ecological conversion,' whereby the effects of their encounter with Jesus Christ become evident in their relationship with the world around them."[68]

Since I became aware of the destructive habits we have adopted into our lifestyles and institutions in modern Western culture, and the way in which these habits imperil the earth and her inhabitants, I have tried to break free of them by implementing changes in my family's routine. To express our love for our common home, we cook more vegetarian meals, shop for gently used clothing instead of new, and tend a garden and compost our scraps, among other things. We have come to prioritize ecological justice as a pro-life issue. It has not been easy—conversion never is. And still, I get overwhelmed when I think of all the habits left to transform. So many of the choices we make are harmful, and I am not confident we will ever succeed in eradicating them from our lifestyle.[69]

And yet—at ages 9, 7, and 5, my kids are more conscious of creation's interconnectedness than I ever was. Recently, for example, they held a bake sale and donated all of their proceeds to the Earth Day Network's Canopy Project, a tree-planting initiative; and my daughter, born on April 22, dedicates part of her celebration every year to honoring her "Earth Day-Birthday" with a clean-up activity. And though they roll their eyes when I recite Mary Oliver as they leave their shoes by the side of the creek and plunge in, their eyes sparkle as if to say, *we're way ahead of you, Mom—here, in this moment, we are living poetry, with our feet buried in mud and our hearts full*

---

65. Brink, *Heavens Are Telling*, 179.

66. See John Paul II, "General Audience," §4.

67. Francis, *Laudato Si'*, §2.

68. Francis, *Laudato Si'*, §217.

69. This and the following paragraphs contain material developed in Bonnette, "No Surprise."

of gratitude. When we leave, we talk about how we can express our thanks, and we find a way to leave the forest healthier than we found it.

It is then that I remember to take the long view. I might not succeed in fully breaking free of habits that oppress our earth rather than love it to flourishing. But just as my parents gave me a foundation for developing ecologically just habits by cultivating in me a love of beauty and the outdoors, so I am passing onto my children those gifts, along with the new practices I am incorporating into our lives. For them, composting will not be a formidable undertaking; it will be part of their homemaking routine, so they will be free to choose new habits that generate life for themselves and their little ones. It still won't be easy, but it will be that much less daunting.

I have been inspired in this approach by the creative efforts of the SSND, who are finding new ways to enfold their charism into the future as they move into a new phase of religious life. Like many congregations of women religious, the SSND are experiencing a transformational shift as their sisters age and there is a decline in new vocations. For many religious communities, changing demographics and varied geographic regions make participation in ministry both a challenge and an opportunity to be creative. The majority of sisters are retired—although, of course, "retired nun" is somewhat of an oxymoron. As Sandra M. Schneiders, IHM, recently noted, "In 1965 there were 180,000 women Religious in the United States, the majority of whom were below the age of 50, and today there are somewhere between 30 and 50 thousand, whose average age is 74."[70] But still, she goes on, we have seen "the emergence, in the same recent time period . . . of a long list of remarkable examples of what women's Religious Life is and fosters and produces."[71]

During my tenure as a staff member in the Atlantic-Midwest Province, the leadership began a campaign called "Embracing the Future," which implemented the discernment and practical process of adapting their community to their current realities. In the midst of the COVID-19 pandemic, they initiated the sale of many of their residential buildings, including the motherhouses and chapels that have seen vows professed for generations. For the sisters, there is heartache as the old way of life fades, but there is hope in the creative energy that draws them forward. Contemplating the hope that manifests in the evolution of ministry and community life is a fruitful exercise for those of us attentive to—and perhaps fearful of—the changes brewing in ecclesial, political, social, and biological life.

70. Schneiders, "Women Erased."

71. Schneiders, "Women Erased."

Throughout this time of change, the sisters in the Atlantic-Midwest engaged in a collaborative dialogue and discernment process as they sought to identify the direction of the province. Despite their grief, they affirmed their desire to be formed in an "integral vision" of cosmology, and they identified five key needs that they committed to serving: addressing climate change, combatting racism, promoting justice for immigrants, ending human trafficking, and working for sustainable development in Haiti. They also pledged to join the *Laudato Si'* Action Platform, which guides them toward full sustainability, "integral ecology," over the next seven years.

The cosmic vision of unity enables the sisters to sit with their grief as they process the losses wrought by change because they know that to continue their mission, they cannot hold tight to the familiar ways of life that no longer work. They are limited now—but aren't we all? Like a mother's love, their gifts are shared through losses that result in stronger bonds.

The SSND are an international congregation with eight distinct provinces around the globe, connected to one another through a Generalate in Rome (as well as various collaborative ministerial projects). And as Ann Scholz, SSND, explained to me, "the gift and challenge of our internationality has formed and reformed us. I believe our history, our experience of the cosmos as it were, has played a critical role in explaining what you experienced of the Atlantic-Midwest Province. The passionate embrace of God's mission to bring all to oneness is baked into our DNA. While that is perhaps the nature of all of God's creation, the SSND experience formed our commitment to unity and our belief that our significant diversity strengthens that commitment."[72]

After their foundation in 1833 by Blessed Theresa of Jesus Gerhardinger in Bavaria, SSND expanded rapidly throughout the world, embodying and carrying forth the charism of unity, primarily through educational initiatives directed toward the empowerment of those made poor and marginalized. Despite the challenges of geographic and cultural distance, the congregation remained connected. For example, Scholz noted, "*You are Sent*, our 1986 constitution and general directory, was written simultaneously in German, the language of our founders, and English, the language of more than half of our members. It was a struggle and a strengthening of our desire to be one congregation, with one rule of life absolutely committed to bringing all to wholeness in the Trinitarian community that is God." Recognizing that "our SSND bonds were tested by two world wars and tried in the fire of the post-Vatican II period of renewal," Scholz emphasized that "the

---

72. I am grateful to Sister Ann for helping me weave my limited experience with that of the broader SSND congregation's. Direct quotes attributed to her here were received in personal correspondence.

wisdom of women committed to the mission of God and the wholeness of the congregation . . . and the grace of Blessed Theresa's initial intent helped us remain one congregation led by women."

Observing their fidelity to tradition, inclusive of the evolutive grace of the Spirit, brings the imaginative richness of cosmology down to a practical level. Indeed, time and again, I watched the sisters relinquish control and entrust their mission to God. Embracing this cosmic consciousness allows for creativity—for allowing limits to be the impetus for new ways of being in the world, new ways of seeking oneness.

As they look toward the future, the SSND in the Atlantic-Midwest Province, for example, maintain sponsored ministries that are staffed predominately by lay people (including programs such as shelters for women, educational programs for immigrants, and educational institutions), and they have partnered with Beyond Borders, an NGO in Haiti that focuses on sustainable development through Model Community Initiatives. To reduce violence, poverty, and child labor and trafficking, and to empower the most vulnerable people to flourish in community, the partnership promotes sustainable livelihoods and education for all. The SSND contribute significant financial resources to the partnership, as well as human resources and expertise. For example, Sharon Slear, SSND, former Provost of Notre Dame of Maryland University, leads a teacher training program to equip teachers on the Haitian island of Lagonav with contemporary teaching techniques to use in the classroom and share with their peers. Though many sisters in the province can no longer offer "boots on the ground," they are finding ways to empower others in mission, instead.

The province also has engaged in initiatives at home to make their residences more eco-friendly, such as installing solar panels, reducing waste and water use, pledging to be a Blue Community that refuses bottled water, and purchasing Fair Trade products when possible. Additionally, they are intentional about managing their investments to ensure that their economic participation is socially responsible and focused on addressing the key concerns of the province. Ethel Howley, SSND, describes how, for example, the efforts of the SSND, as members of the Interfaith Center on Corporate Responsibility, "persuaded J. P. Morgan Chase to withdraw from funding privately owned prisons used for immigrant families."[73] She explains: "Through engagements with the world's largest corporations, SSND are attempting to address the current world's ecological hurdles and social challenges, which include the basic rights of the poor and

73. Howley, "Four Commitments."

underprivileged. We believe that we have a shared responsibility for others and the care of all creation."[74]

This, of course, begins with prayer, which, when genuine, always directs our attention toward the whole. Once, while working for the SSND, I wrote a call to action for the community concerning the right of refugees to access clean water. In it, I included a prayer that began with a petition for God to bless those who are thirsty, and to provide them with clean water sources. A few days later, I received a phone call from one of the sisters, who told me—in no uncertain terms—that she disapproved of this prayer. "When we pray," she insisted, "we should ask the Spirit to move *us* to action. God is not a fix-all cure; we are the embodiment of the loving energy that is God." Her words resonate with those attributed to Saint Mother Teresa of Calcutta: "I used to pray that God would feed the hungry, or do this or that, but now I pray that [God] will guide me to do whatever I'm supposed to do, what I can do. I used to pray for answers, but now I'm praying for strength. I used to believe that prayer changes things, but now I know that prayer changes us and we change things." In this, I hear echoes, too, of Augustine's view of "cooperative grace," reflected in his translation of Romans 8:28—"God, along with those who love [God], works everything for the good."[75] The Spirit moves only as far as we are willing to go.

The current Directional Statement of the SSND, the document that offers a framework for action to the Congregation for a given number of years, is entitled *Love Gives Everything*; it is based on the wisdom of their founder, Blessed Theresa, who emphasized, "Love gives everything gladly, everything again and again, daily."[76] In their special concern for persons who are poor, the SSND embody their Augustinian roots: "See where love begins," Augustine writes. "If you're not yet capable of [perfect love], be capable even now of giving [your neighbor] some of your goods. Let love stir your heart to action now."[77]

As the SSND and women religious throughout the world accompany those who are marginalized, suffer the changes of time, and create new ways to embody and hand on their charism, we see the cosmic spirituality that finds the incarnation, passion, and resurrection of Christ enacted over and over again in the work of loving the world. Virginia Brien, SSND, summed it up nicely with an unintentional metaphor when she reflected on her participation in a bag swap project, for which she sewed a slew of reusable grocery

74. Howley, "Investors."

75. Augustine, "On Grace and Free Choice," 17.33, in *On the Free Choice*.

76. Gerhardinger, "Letter: Stadtamhof," in Kuttner, *Sowing the Seed*, 1.

77. Augustine, *Love One Another*, 52.

bags for local shoppers: "I have so much material that was given to me to do something with,"[78] the ninety-four year old said simply.

We evolve, together, and each of us affects the future, though we are not singularly responsible for it. Love weaves a grand tapestry.

PAUSE FOR REFLECTION

Take a moment to reflect on what you read.

- What is drawing your attention? What words, phrases, or concepts stand out to you? Are any new insights stirring in you?

- Why is it important to shift the paradigm of finding God from ascent to encounter? Do you feel resistant to a paradigm shift? Why?

- What might it mean to adopt the "transformational values" of both/ and thinking, a mindset of abundance, open dialogue, and communitarian systems? How might your life change?

78. Haines, "Baltimore School Sisters."

Conclusion

Toward Wholeness

As I begin to wind down this personal, theological exploration, I confess that my mind is scattered. In the past three weeks, there have been two high-profile mass shootings—one racially motivated, one targeting elementary school students; the Supreme Court overturned *Roe v. Wade* and made it possible for abortion to be banned with no exceptions—an outcome that has been pursued as morally necessary by the church, but which, in a clear example of the ambiguity of moral action, has been obtained by propping up the political party that has missed the mark egregiously on pro-life matters, from denying the insidious presence of racism in America, to gutting or blocking social protection measures (including commonsense gun safety laws); Archbishop Cordileone of San Francisco publicly barred Speaker of the House Nancy Pelosi from receiving the Eucharist because of her advocacy for abortion rights (not, we should note, for abortion itself), highlighting inconsistency and division within the church, as well as the deep-seated tension between the male clerical hierarchy and Catholic women; and Russia has been waging war in Ukraine.

We are still too far behind in addressing climate change; gun violence and drug overdoses occur in epidemic proportions; a global pandemic is ongoing; and migrants and refugees at our southern border and around the globe are still waiting for welcome as they flee violence and poverty. By the time you read this, I assume you will have more tragic aggressions to add to this list.

Meanwhile, I am safe with my family in our comfortable home in the suburbs, where I have had the luxury of spending the past semester writing this book, and our whiteness insulates us from most of these worries. We are celebrating the end of the school year and planning a family vacation.

I confess that I do not know how to hold all of this in my heart. The anger, grief, and despair; the joyful energy. The awareness of such vast inequality; the enjoyment of privilege. I am not sure where to go from here.

And yet—if the spirituality that is emerging from the reflective exercise that I have undertaken in this project is to have any meaning whatsoever, isn't it precisely now, when the tensions and contradictions are so fraught, the suffering so palpable, the dominative paradigm so apparent?

The cosmos has been evolving since the beginning of time, moving with grace through turmoil, from which emerges new life. Entities pass away, only to be carried forward in new relationships and ways of being, forever contained in the consciousness of the universe. The weaving God draws all into wholeness; the cosmic Christ holds all.

My response, then, cannot be to retreat into myself, as I am wont to do with emotions as heavy as this. Can I learn instead to embody my cosmological roots by reaching out to form and strengthen relationships? Nurturing my garden and receiving the gift of its sustenance; opening my home to refugee children; baking cookies for my neighbors; helping people register to vote; teaching my kids to read; laughing with my husband; sipping tea and playing Scrabble with my parents: these actions will never mend what has been broken, but they channel, in small ways, the energy of love. As earth, conscious of itself, my responses serve to carry the world forward by embracing the lessons of the past—even if I feel ineffective; even if I am imperfect.

I could succumb to despair. I could throw up my hands, accept the suffering in the world, and enjoy my own privilege—praying and waiting for the perfection of another world, or simply getting all I can out of this one. Despair stops us in our tracks, but the Spirit moves.

The energy of love moves us out of nothing toward the fullness of the cosmic Christ. The hope of wholeness, toward which we see the world moving, can draw us from the nothingness of despair, from the nihilism of selfishness. It can draw us through suffering, into new life, as we work to carry the world toward its purpose: "that all will be one."

So, what do I love when I love my God? The answer remains elusive. But I look toward the horizons with hope.

Bibliography

Alexander VI. *Inter Caetera*. Papal Bull on the Division of the Undiscovered World between Spain and Portugal. May 4, 1493.

Armstrong, A. H., ed. *The Cambridge History of Later Greek and Early Medieval Philosophy*. Cambridge: Cambridge University Press, 1967.

Augustine. *Augustine: Political Writings*. Edited by E. M. Atkins and R. J. Dodaro. Cambridge: Cambridge University Press, 2001.

———. *City of God*. Translated by Henry Battenson. Edited by David Knowles. Harmondsworth, UK: Pelican Classics, 1972.

———. *Confessions*. Translated by R. S. Pine-Coffin. London: Penguin Classics, 1961.

———. *Confessions*. Translated by Sarah Ruden. New York: Modern Library, 2018.

———. *Eighty-three Different Questions: A New Translation*. Translated by David L. Mosher. The Fathers of the Church 70. Washington, DC: Catholic University of America Press, 1982.

———. *Essential Expositions of the Psalms by Saint Augustine*. Edited by Boniface Ramsey. Translated by Maria Boulding. The Works of Saint Augustine: A Translation for the 21st Century. Hyde Park, NY: New City, 2015.

———. *Essential Sermons*. Edited by Boniface Ramsey. Translated by Edmund Hill. The Works of Saint Augustine: A Translation for the 21st Century. Hyde Park, NY: New City, 2007.

———. *Love One Another, My Friends: St. Augustine's Homilies on the First Letter of John*. Translated by John Leinenweber. San Francisco, CA: Harper and Row, 1989.

———. *On Christian Doctrine*. Translated by James Shaw. Nicene and Post-Nicene Fathers, First Series, Vol. 2. Edited by Philip Schaff. Buffalo, NY: Christian Literature, 1887. Revised and edited for New Advent by Kevin Knight. http://www.newadvent.org/fathers/1202.htm.

———. *On the Free Choice of the Will, On Grace and Free Choice, and Other Writings*. Translated by Peter King. Cambridge: Cambridge University Press, 2010.

———. *On Genesis: Two Books on Genesis against the Manichees and On the Literal Interpretation of Genesis: An Unfinished Book*. Translated by Roland J. Teske. The Fathers of the Church: A New Translation 84. Washington, DC: The Catholic University of America Press, 1991.

———. *On the Morals of the Catholic Church*. Translated by Richard Stothert. Nicene and Post-Nicene Fathers, First Series, Vol. 4. Edited by Philip Schaff. Buffalo, NY: Christian Literature, 1887. Revised and edited for New Advent by Kevin Knight. http://www.newadvent.org/fathers/1401.htm.

———. *On the Trinity: Books 8–15*. Edited by Gareth B. Matthews. Translated by Stephen McKenna. Cambridge Texts in the History of Philosophy. Cambridge: Cambridge University Press, 2002.

———. *Sermons*. Edited by John E. Rotelle. Translated by Edmund Hill. Vol. III: Sermons 51–94. The Works of Saint Augustine: A Translation for the 21st Century. Brooklyn, NY: New City, 1991.

———. *Tractates on the Gospel of John*. Translated by John Gibb. Nicene and Post-Nicene Fathers, First Series, Vol. 7. Edited by Philip Schaff. Buffalo, NY: Christian Literature, 1888. Revised and edited for New Advent by Kevin Knight. http://www.newadvent.org/fathers/1701050.htm.

Barrows, Isabel C., ed. *Proceedings of the National Conference of Charities and Correction*. Denver, CO: 1892.

Bohm, David. *Unfolding Meaning: A Weekend of Dialogue with David Bohm*. London: Routledge, 1985.

Bonilla-Silva, Eduardo. *Racism without Racists: Color-blind Racism and the Persistence of Racial Inequality in America*. 5th ed. Lanham: Rowman & Littlefield, 2018.

Bonnette, Kathleen. "A Branch Regrafted: An Augustinian Approach to Restorative Justice." *Journal of Catholic Social Thought* 15.1 (Winter 2018) 181–210.

———. "Catholics: Embrace Being 'Woke.' It's Part of Our Faith Tradition." *America: The Jesuit Review*, May 26, 2021. https://www.americamagazine.org/politics-society/2021/05/26/wokeness-pastoral-cycle-see-judge-act-240639.

———. "'Habits of the Flesh' and the Call to Conversion: How Augustinian Ecology Can Illuminate Justice in the World." *Journal of Catholic Social Thought* 18.2 (Summer 2021) 227–40.

———. "The Heart of Justice: An Augustinian Ethic of Relational Responsibility." ThD Diss., La Salle University, 2016.

———. "No Surprise: Nuns Are Taking the Lead in Putting 'Laudato Si" into Action." *America: The Jesuit Review*, July 6, 2021. https://www.americamagazine.org/faith/2021/07/06/women-religious-laudato-si-school-sisters-notre-dame-240958.

———. "Now Is the Time for a New Catholic Political Vision." *U.S. Catholic*, September 10, 2020. https://uscatholic.org/articles/202009/now-is-the-time-for-a-new-catholic-political-vision/.

———. "Oscar Romero Stood with the Marginalized. Christ Does Too." *U.S. Catholic*, March 24, 2021. https://uscatholic.org/articles/202103/oscar-romero-stood-with-the-marginalized-christ-does-too/.

———. "Partnership as a Model for Mission: Lessons on Solidarity from Augustine and the School Sisters of Notre Dame." *Praxis: An Interdisciplinary Journal of Faith and Justice* 2.1 (2019) 3–22.

———. "Where Do We Go from Here? My Post-Election Confessions." *Millennial*, December 23, 2020. https://millennialjournal.com/2020/12/23/where-do-we-go-from-here-my-post-election-confessions/.

Bowman, Donna, and Clayton Crockett, eds. *Cosmology, Ecology, and the Energy of God*. New York: Fordham University Press, 2012.

Bowman, Thea. "Sr. Thea Bowman's Address to the U.S. Bishop's Conference." Speech, June 1989. https://www.usccb.org/issues-and-action/cultural-diversity/african-american/resources/upload/Transcript-Sr-Thea-Bowman-June-1989-Address.pdf.

Brink, Laurie. *The Heavens Are Telling the Glory of God: An Emerging Chapter for Religious Life; Science, Theology, and Mission.* Collegeville, MN: Liturgical, 2022.

Brown, Peter. *Augustine of Hippo: A Biography.* 45th anniversary ed. Berkeley: University of California Press, 2000.

Brueggemann, Walter. "How to Read the Bible on Homosexuality." Outreach: An LGBTQ Catholic Resource. *America Media*, September 4, 2022. https://outreach.faith/2022/09/walter-brueggemann-how-to-read-the-bible-on-homosexuality/.

Camacho, Paul. "The Weight of Love: Augustine on Desire and the Limits of Autonomy." PhD Diss., Villanova University, 2016.

Camacho, Paul, and Ian Clausen, eds. *Studia Patristica*, Vol. CXVI: Papers Presented at the Eighteenth International Conference on Patristic Studies, Oxford 2019. Volume 13: *Ordo Amoris*. Leuven: Peeters, 2021.

Cannato, Judy. *Field of Compassion: How the New Cosmology Is Transforming Spiritual Life.* Notre Dame, IN: Sorin, 2010.

Caputo, John D., and Michael J. Scanlon, eds. *Augustine and Postmodernism: Confession and Circumfession.* Bloomington: Indiana University Press, 2004.

Carey, Ann. "Women Religious and the New Cosmology." *National Catholic Register*, February 18, 2014. https://www.ncregister.com/commentaries/women-religious-and-the-new-cosmology.

Catholic Church. *Catechism of the Catholic Church.* Vatican City: Libreria Editrice Vaticana, 1994.

Chadwick, Henry. Introduction to *Saint Augustine's Confessions: A New Translation by Henry Chadwick.* Oxford World's Classics. Oxford: Oxford University Press, 1992.

Citron-Fink, Ronnie. "One Mom's Story from the Frontlines of the Dakota Access Pipeline Resistance." Moms Clean Air Force, October 31, 2016, https://www.momscleanairforce.org/native-moms-story-dakota-pipeline/.

Clair, Joseph. *Discerning the Good in the Letters and Sermons of Augustine.* Oxford: Oxford University Press, 2016.

Clark, Fred. "Ignorant Christians need to STFU about 'The Poor You Will Always Have With You' Until They Can Be Bothered to Understand What Jesus Actually Said." *Patheos*, December 10, 2014. https://www.patheos.com/blogs/slacktivist/2014/12/10/ignorant-christians-need-to-stfu-about-the-poor-you-will-always-have-with-you-until-they-can-be-bothered-to-understand-what-jesus-actually-said/.

Clausen, Ian. *On Love, Confession, Surrender and the Moral Self.* Reading Augustine. New York: Bloomsbury Academic, 2018.

Congregation for the Doctrine of the Faith. "Doctrinal Assessment of the Leadership Conference of Women Religious." April 18, 2012. https://www.vatican.va/roman_curia/congregations/cfaith/documents/rc_con_cfaith_doc_20120418_assessment-lcwr_en.html.

———. "*Inter Insigniores*: On the Question of Admission of Women to the Ministerial Priesthood." October 15, 1976. https://www.vatican.va/roman_curia/congregations/cfaith/documents/rc_con_cfaith_doc_19761015_inter-insigniores_en.html.

———. "Letter to the Bishops of the Catholic Church on Some Aspects of the Church Understood as Communion." May 28, 1992. https://www.vatican.va/roman_curia/

congregations/cfaith/documents/rc_con_cfaith_doc_28051992_communionis-notio_en.html.

Congregation for the Doctrine of the Faith and Leadership Conference of Women Religious. "Joint Final Report on the Doctrinal Assessment of the Leadership Conference of Women Religious (LCWR) by the Congregation for the Doctrine of the Faith (CDF)." April 16, 2015. https://press.vatican.va/content/salastampa/it/bollettino/pubblico/2015/04/16/0278/00618.html.

Copeland, M. Shawn. *Enfleshing Freedom: Body, Race, and Being.* Minneapolis: Fortress, 2009.

———, ed. *Uncommon Faithfulness: The Black Catholic Experience.* Maryknoll, NY: Orbis, 2009.

Danielewicz, Noel, OFM. "Thea Bowman & Bede Abram." *Franciscan Voice,* February 4, 2021. https://franciscanvoice.org/thea-bowman-bede-abram/.

Dávila, MT. "The Challenge of a 'Preferential Option' to Faith in a Context of Privilege." Abstract. https://www.luc.edu/media/lucedu/ccih/formsdocumentsandpdfs/Latin CultureTheology.BioAndAbstract.MariaTeresaDavila.pdf.

Delio, Ilia. *Making All Things New: Catholicity, Cosmology, and Consciousness.* Catholicity in an Evolving Universe. Maryknoll, NY: Orbis, 2015.

DelRosso, Jeana, ed. *Unruly Catholic Nuns: Sisters' Stories.* Albany: State University of New York Press, 2017.

Desmond, William. "Companioning." *On the Way With Augustine.* The Augustine Blog, 2022. https://augustineblog.com/companioning/.

Editors of *America: The Jesuit Review.* "The Catholic Church Must Come Clean—Completely—About What It Did to Native Americans." *America: The Jesuit Review,* June 30, 2021. https://www.americamagazine.org/politics-society/2021/06/30/native-american-boarding-schools-catholic-church-investigation-240950.

Editors of *National Catholic Reporter.* "Ivone Gebara Must Be Doing Something Right." *National Catholic Reporter,* August 25, 1995. https://www.thefreelibrary.com/Ivone+Gebara+must+be+doing+something+right.-a017288427.

Eisler, Riane. "The Dynamics of Cultural and Technological Evolution: Domination versus Partnership." *World Futures: The Journal of General Evolution* 58.2 (2002) 159–74.

Farrell, Pat. "Stay the Course of Contemplation." *Update: A Publication of the Leadership Conference of Women Religious,* July 2012.

Ferris, Susanne Sartor. "The Bible on Steroids: The Effect of Androcentrism on the Lectionary." *New Theology Review* 15.1 (February 2002) 21–31.

Fitzgerald, Allan, ed. *Augustine through the Ages: An Encyclopedia.* Grand Rapids, MI: W. B. Eerdmans, 1999.

Flaherty, Arlene. "Introduction." Integral Vision Series. School Sisters of Notre Dame, Atlantic-Midwest Province, 2019. https://atlanticmidwest.org/integral-vision-series.

Flaherty, Arlene, et al. "We Have Family in Iraq: A Journey in Solidarity and Love." Global Sisters Report. *National Catholic Reporter,* January 4, 2015. https://www.globalsistersreport.org/column/justice-matters/equality/we-have-family-iraq-journey-solidarity-and-love-17501.

Francis I. "Homily on Pentecost Sunday." St. Peter's Basilica, Vatican City, May 31, 2020. https://www.catholicnewsagency.com/news/44696/full-text-pope-francis-homily-on-pentecost-sunday.

————. *Laudato Si'*. Encyclical Letter on Care for Our Common Home. Vatican, May 24, 2015. http://w2.vatican.va/content/francesco/en/encyclicals/documents/papa -francesco_20150524_enciclica-laudato-si.html.

————. "Message for the 5th World Day of the Poor." *CBCP News*, June 13, 2021, https:// cbcpnews.net/cbcpnews/pope-francis-message-for-the-5th-world-day-of-the- poor/.

Francis I and Austen Ivereigh. *Let Us Dream: The Path to a Better Future*. London: Simon and Schuster, 2020.

Garrett, Josephine. "Martin Luther King Jr. Was Right: We Must Not Choose Order Over Justice." *America: The Jesuit Review*, February 2022. https://www.americamagazine. org/faith/2022/01/14/black-history-month-justice-mlk-242174.

Gebara, Ivone. "Ecofeminism: A Latin American Perspective." *Cross Currents* 531 (Spring 2003) 93–103.

Georgetown University: Initiative on Catholic Social Thought and Public Life. "Sister Thea Bowman: Faithful Life, Powerful Legacy, Continuing Lessons." Video. May 3, 2022. https://catholicsocialthought.georgetown.edu/events/sister-thea-bowman.

Gilligan, Carol. *The Deepening Darkness: Patriarchy, Resistance, and Democracy's Future*. Cambridge: Cambridge University Press, 2009.

Gordon, Mary. "Francis and the Nuns: Is the New Vatican All Talk?" *Harper's Magazine*, August 2014. https://harpers.org/archive/2014/08/francis-and-the-nuns/.

Gross, Terry. "An American Nun Responds to Vatican Criticism." *NPR Fresh Air*, July 17, 2012. https://www.npr.org/2012/07/17/156858223/an-american-nun-responds -to-vatican-condemnation.

Haines, Caelie. "Baltimore School Sisters of Notre Dame, NDP Students, and Staff Promote Green Habits." Global Sisters Report. *National Catholic Reporter*, December 19, 2019. https://www.globalsistersreport.org/community/news/baltimore-school- sisters-notre-dame-ndp-students-and-staff-promote-green-habits.

Hall, Heidi. "Sister Elizabeth Johnson: 'The Waste of Time on This Investigation Is Uncon- scionable.'" *Religion News Service*, August 16, 2014. https://religionnews.com/2014 /08/16/sister-elizabeth-johnson-waste-time-investigation-unconscionable/.

Hampson, Peter J., and Johannes Hoff. "Whose Self? Which Unification? Augustine's Anthropology and the Psychology-Theology Debate." *New Blackfriars* (2010) 546–66.

Harjo, Joy. *A Map to the Next World: Poems and Tales*. New York: W. W. Norton, 2000.

————. *She Had Some Horses*. New York: W. W. Norton, 1983.

Hayes, Diana L. *And Still We Rise: An Introduction to Black Liberation Theology*. New York: Paulist, 1996.

Henderson, J. Frank, ed. *Remembering the Women: Women's Stories from Scripture for Sundays and Festivals*. Chicago: Liturgy Training, 1999.

hooks, bell. *The Will to Change: Men, Masculinity, and Love*. New York: Washington Square, 2005.

Howley, Ethel. "The Four Commitments, Integral Ecology, and SSNDs." School Sisters of Notre Dame, March 2019. https://atlanticmidwest.org/posts/four-commitments- integral-ecology-and-ssnds.

————. "Investors, Climate Change, and Human Rights." School Sisters of Notre Dame, n.d. https://atlanticmidwestssnd.org/posts/investors-climate-change-and-human-rights.

Intergovernmental Panel on Climate Change. "Special Report: Global Warming of 1.5 °C." 2018. https://www.ipcc.ch/sr15/.

Isasi-Díaz, Ada Maria, and Eduardo Mendieta, eds. *Decolonizing Epistemologies:Latina/o Theology and Philosophy*. Transdisciplinary Theological Colloquia. New York: Fordham University Press, 2012.

John Paul II. *Fides et Ratio.* Encyclical Letter on Faith and Reason. Vatican, September 14, 1998. https://www.vatican.va/content/john-paul-ii/en/encyclicals/documents/hf_jp-ii_enc_14091998_fides-et-ratio.html.

———. "General Audience: God Made Man the Steward of Creation." Vatican, January 17, 2001. https://www.vatican.va/content/john-paul-ii/en/audiences/2001/documents/hf_jp-ii_aud_20010117.html.

———. *Ordinatio Sacerdotalis.* Apostolic Letter to the Bishops of the Catholic Church on Reserving Priestly Ordination to Men Alone. Vatican, May 22, 1994. https://www.vatican.va/content/john-paul-ii/en/apost_letters/1994/documents/hf_jp-ii_apl_19940522_ordinatio-sacerdotalis.html.

Johnson, Elizabeth A. *Ask the Beasts: Darwin and the God of Love*. London: Bloomsbury, 2014.

———. *She Who Is: The Mystery of God in Feminist Theological Discourse*. 25th anniversary ed. Chestnut Ridge, PA: Crossroad, 2017.

Kearns, Laurel, and Catherine Keller, eds. *Ecospirit: Religions and Philosophies for the Earth*. Transdisciplinary Theological Colloquia. New York: Fordham University Press, 2007.

Kelly, Jean P. "Untold Stories: Is It Time to Update Mass Readings in the Lectionary?" *US Catholic* 84.6 (June 2019) 33–36.

Kidwell, Clara Sue, et al. *A Native American Theology*. Maryknoll, NY: Orbis, 2001.

Kimmerer, Robin Wall. *Braiding Sweetgrass: Indigenous Wisdom, Scientific Knowledge, and the Teachings of Plants*. Minneapolis, MN: Milkweed, 2013.

Kuttner, Mary Ann, ed. *Sowing the Seed, 1822–1840*. Letters of Mary Theresa of Jesus Gerhardinger: Foundress of the School Sisters of Notre Dame 1. Elm Grove, WI: School Sisters of Notre Dame, 2010.

Leadership Conference of Women Religious. "Book Announcement." LCWR. https://lcwr.org/resources/publications/however-long-the-night.

Ledoux, Arthur O. "A Green Augustine: On Learning to Love Nature Well." *Theology and Science* 3.3 (2005) 331–44.

Lerner, Gerda. *The Creation of Patriarchy*. Women and History 1. New York: Oxford University Press, 1986.

Lienhard, Joseph T., et al., eds. *Augustine: Presbyter Factus Sum*. Collectanea Augustiniana. New York: Peter Lang, 1993.

Mascarenhas, Mridula. "Prophetic and Deliberative Responses to the Doctrinal Voice: A Study of the Rhetorical Engagement between Catholic Nuns and Church Hierarchy." *Journal of Communication & Religion* 39.4 (Winter 2017) 36–54.

Maya, Teresa. "A Vision for the Future of Religious Life." Address, International Union of Superiors General, Rome, 2019.

Meconi, David, ed. *Augustine's Confessions and Contemporary Concerns*. St. Paul, MN: Saint Paul Seminary Press, 2022.

Medina, Lara. *Las Hermanas: Chicana/Latina Religious-Political Activism in the U.S. Catholic Church*. Philadelphia: Temple University Press, 2004.

Miles, Tiya. *All That She Carried: The Journey of Ashley's Sack, a Black Family Keepsake*. New York: Random House, 2021.

Miller, Richard B. "Evil, Friendship, and Iconic Realism in Augustine's Confessions." *Harvard Theological Review* 104.4 (October 2011) 387–409.

Muzaffar, Maroosha. "Marjorie Taylor Greene Mocked Over Her Definition of a Woman—the 'Weaker Sex' Created from Adam's Rib." *The Independent*, April 05, 2022. https://www.independent.co.uk/news/world/americas/us-politics/marjorie -taylor-greene-definition-woman-b2051323.html.

Niebuhr, H. Richard. *The Responsible Self: An Essay in Christian Moral Philosophy.* Library of Theological Ethics. Louisville, KY: Westminster John Knox, 1999. First published 1963 by Harper and Row.

Nightingale, Andrea. *Once Out of Nature: Augustine on Time and the Body.* Chicago: University of Chicago Press, 2011.

O'Connell, Kay. "Reflections on Integral Ecology." *Get WITH It*, May 24, 2019. https:// atlanticmidwest.org/posts/get-it-may-24th.

O'Donovan, Oliver. *The Problem of Self-Love in St. Augustine.* Eugene, OR: Wipf and Stock, 1980.

Ogle, Veronica. *Politics and the Earthly City in Augustine's City of God.* Cambridge: Cambridge University Press, 2020.

Oliver, Mary. *Evidence.* Boston: Beacon, 2009.

Oluo, Ijeoma. *So You Want to Talk About Race.* First ed. New York: Seal, 2018.

Ortiz, Dianna. *The Blindfold's Eyes: My Journey from Torture to Truth.* Maryknoll, NY: Orbis, 2002.

Ouellet, Marc, ed. *For a Fundamental Theology of the Priesthood.* Rome: Libreria Editrice Vaticana, 2022.

Paul VI. *Populorum progressio*, encyclical. Vatican, March 26, 1967. http://www.vati can.va/content/paul-vi/en/encyclicals/documents/hf_p-vi_enc_26031967_popu lorum.html.

Peppard, Michael. "Household Names: Junia, Phoebe, & Prisca in Early Christian Rome." *Commonweal Magazine*, April 23, 2018. https://www.commonwealmagazine.org/ household-names.

Pramuk, Christopher. *Hope Sings, So Beautiful: Graced Encounters across the Color Line.* Collegeville, MN: Liturgical, 2013.

Puelo, Mey. *The Struggle Is One: Voices and Visions of Liberation.* Albany: State University of New York Press, 1994.

Ress, Mary Judith. "Interview with Brazilian Feminist Theologian Ivone Gebara." *Feminist Theology* 3.8 (1995) 107–16.

Rolheiser, Ronald. *Against an Infinite Horizon: The Finger of God in Our Everyday Lives.* Rev. ed. New York: Crossroad, 2001. First published 1995 by Hodder & Stroughton.

Russell, Heidi. *The Source of All Love: Catholicity and the Trinity.* Catholicity in an Evolving Universe. Maryknoll, NY: Orbis, 2017.

Sanders, Annmarie, ed. *However Long the Night: Making Meaning in a Time of Crisis.* Silver Springs, MD: Leadership Conference of Women Religious, 2018.

Schlabach, Gerald W. "'Love Is the Hand of the Soul': The Grammar of Continence in Augustine's Doctrine of Christian Love." *Journal of Early Christian Studies* 6.1 (1998) 59–92.

Schneiders, Sandra. "Women Erased: Catholic Women, Feminism, and a New Paradigm for Being Church with Sr. Sandra Schneiders, IHM." Future Church, April 21, 2021. https://futurechurch.org/women-in-church-leadership/new-paradigm/.

School Sisters of Notre Dame. *You Are Sent: Constitution and General Directory of the School Sisters of Notre Dame*. Milwaukee, WI, 1986.

Schrader, Elizabeth, and Joan E. Taylor. "The Meaning of 'Magdalene': A Review of Literary Evidence." *Journal of Biblical Literature* 140.4 (2021) 751–73.

Second Vatican Council. Pastoral Constitution *Gaudium et spes*. Dec. 7, 1965. Holy See. https://www.vatican.va/archive/hist_councils/ii_vatican_council/documents/vat-ii_const_19651207_gaudium-et-spes_en.html.

Stark, Judith Chelius, ed. *Feminist Interpretations of Augustine*. Re-reading the Canon. University Park: The Pennsylvania State University Press, 2007.

Teresa of Ávila. *The Way of Perfection*. Translated by E. Allison Peers. London: Sheed and Ward, 1946.

Vacek, Edward Collins. *Love, Human and Divine: The Heart of Christian Ethics*. Washington, DC: Georgetown University Press, 1994.

Vatican Press Office. "Press Release on the Final Report Regarding the Implementation of the LCWR Doctrinal Assessment and Mandate of April 2012 by CDF." April 16, 2015. https://press.vatican.va/content/salastampa/it/bollettino/pubblico/2015/04/16/0278/00617.html.

Wetzel, James. *Parting Knowledge: Essays after Augustine*. Eugene, OR: Cascade, 2013.

Williams, Shannen Dee. "Black Catholic Women like Amanda Gorman Are Forgotten Prophets of American Democracy." *The Washington Post*, February 10, 2021. https://www.washingtonpost.com/outlook/2021/02/10/black-catholic-women-are-forgotten-prophets-american-democracy/.

———. "I Wrote the First Full History of Black Catholic Nuns in the US. Here's What I Learned." *America: The Jesuit Review*, March 31, 2022.

———. *Subversive Habits: Black Catholic Nuns in the Long African American Freedom Struggle*. Durham: Duke University Press, 2022.

Zafeiris, Anna, and Tamás Vicsek. *Why We Live in Hierarchies? A Quantitative Treatise*. SpringerBriefs in Complexity. Cham: Springer, 2018.

Zohar, Danah. *The Quantum Self: Human Nature and Consciousness Defined by the New Physics*. New York: William Morrow, 1990.

Made in United States
North Haven, CT
09 July 2024

54559176R00093